WRITERS AND THEIR WORK

ISOBEL ARMSTRONG
General Editor

NEIL M. GUNN

NEIL GUNN

NEIL M. GUNN

J. B. Pick

Northcote House
in association with the
British Council

© Copyright 2004 by J. B. Pick

First published in 2004 by Northcote House Publishers Ltd, Horndon, Tavistock, Devon, PL19 9NQ, United Kingdom.
Tel: +44 (0) 1822 810066 Fax: +44 (0) 1822 810034.

British Library Cataloguing-in-Publication Data
A catalogue record for this book is available from the British Library

ISBN 0-7463-1120-6 hardback
ISBN 0-7463-0989-9 paperback

Typeset by PDQ Typesetting, Newcastle-under-Lyme
Printed and bound in the United Kingdom by Athenaeum Press Ltd., Gateshead

In memory of
FRANCIS RUSSELL HART
who died before he could advise me
how to improve this book.

Contents

Acknowledgements

I want to thank Dr John Burns for his valuable help and advice in the preparation of this book; Dairmid Gunn for allowing me a free hand in quotation; Souvenir Press for permission to quote from *Bloodhunt*, *Butcher's Broom*, *The Green Isle of the Great Deep*, and *Morning Tide*; Faber & Faber, from *The Silver Darlings*; Canongate, from *Highland River*, *The Key of the Chest*, *The Serpent*, *Sun Circle*, and *The Well at the World's End*; Polygon, from *The Atom of Delight* and *Selected Letters*; and the House of Lochar, from *Off in a Boat* and *The Other Landscape*.

I would like, too, to acknowledge John Murray, Canongate, Polygon, and Chambers, the publishers of previous efforts I have made to do justice to Gunn in biography, essays and introductions.

Biographical Outline

1891   Neil Miller Gunn born on 8 November in Dunbeath, Caithness.

1903   Went to stay with sister Mary and her doctor husband at St John's Town of Dalry, Galloway. Studied for Civil Service entrance examination.

1907   Passed entrance exam.

1907–9   Worked with Civil Service in London.

1909–11   Civil Servant in Edinburgh.

1911–21   Excise officer travelling the Highlands 'on supply'. Met Maurice Walsh. During the war stationed at Kinlochleven routeing ships round minefields. Began to write poems, essays and short stories.

1921   Assigned to a post in Wigan. Married Jessie Frew (known as 'Daisy').

1922   Assigned to Lybster, Caithness. Maurice Walsh returned to Ireland and the two men challenged each other to write.

1923   Transferred to Inverness as officer in residence, Glen Mhor distillery.

1926   Built Inverness bungalow 'Larachan'. First novel, 'The Grey Coast', published.

1929   National Party of Scotland founded. Gunn joined at its first Inverness meeting, and his house became a centre for discussion and planning.

1931   *Morning Tide* became a Book Society Choice and a commercial and critical success. John McCormick stood as National Party candidate in Inverness.

1932   Became a member of National Council of the party. Prime mover in negotiations between National Party and Scottish Party to form a united Scottish National

Party. This is the probable period for the accident which caused Daisy to miscarry. As a result there was estrangement for several years.

1934   Trip to Spain during which Gunn almost drowned.

1937   *Highland River* won James Tait Black Memorial Prize. Gunn resigned from Civil Service to write full-time.

1938   Bought a boat and sailed down west coast, visiting the Isles. Rented Braefarm House, near Dingwall.

1939   Kept a journal during this year, describing his uneasy state of mind with war imminent.

1941–5   During the war years wrote and published several of his best novels: *The Silver Darlings* (1941), *Young Art and Old Hector* (1942), *The Serpent* (1943), *The Green Isle of the Great Deep* (1944), *The Key of the Chest* (1945).

1942–3   Member of Committee of Enquiry into post-war hospital requirements for Scotland.

1948   Honorary LLD from Edinburgh University.

1949   Moved to 'Kincraig', overlooking Cromarty Firth.

1951   Gunn's friend James Bridie died and he ceased regular attendance at British Council meetings, where they had often met.

1951–4   Member of Committee of Enquiry into crofting conditions.

1951   Moved to Kerrow House, Cannich, near Glen Affric.

1952   *Bloodhunt* published. Served on Highlands and Islands Film Council.

1953   Daisy became ill.

1954   Gunn began to suffer from acute facial neuralgia, anaemia and low blood pressure, with loss of energy. Depressed by the adverse reception of *The Other Landscape*, his last novel.

1956   Final book, the elusive spiritual autobiography *The Atom of Delight* published but largely ignored.

1958–9   Wrote several philosophical articles for the *Saltire Review*.

1960   Moved to 'Dalcraig' on the Black Isle, Easter Ross.

1962   Member of group applying for programme control of Caledonian Television. Acted as adviser for Seager Evans and Co. in their search for a new distillery – Tormore. Serious prostate operation in Edinburgh.

1963   Daisy Gunn died.

1964   Visit to Gran Canaria with Neil and Rose Paterson, the first of several trips to Spain, Portugal, the Canaries. Maurice Walsh died.

1967–8   Copyright for out-of-print books regained from Faber. Too late.

1973   Neil Gunn died on 15 January.

Abbreviations

AD	*The Atom of Delight* (London: Faber & Faber, 1956)
B	*Bloodhunt* (London: Faber & Faber, 1952)
BB	*Butcher's Broom* (Edinburgh: Porpoise Press, 1934)
DW	*The Drinking Well* (London: Faber & Faber, 1946)
GC	*The Grey Coast* (London: Jonathan Cape, 1926)
GI	*The Green Isle of the Great Deep* (London: Faber & Faber, 1944)
HD	*Hidden Doors* (Edinburgh: Porpoise Press, 1929)
HP	*Highland Pack* (London: Faber & Faber, 1949)
HR	*Highland River* (Edinburgh: Porpoise Press, 1937)
KC	*The Key of the Chest* (London: Faber & Faber, 1945)
LC	*The Lost Chart* (London: Faber & Faber, 1949)
LG	*The Lost Glen* (Edinburgh: Porpoise Press, 1932)
MT	*Morning Tide* (Edinburgh: Porpoise Press, 1931)
OB	*Off in a Boat* (London: Faber & Faber, 1938)
OL	*The Other Landscape* (London: Faber & Faber, 1954)
S	*The Serpent* (Edinburgh: Canongate Classics, 1997)
SB	*The Silver Bough* (London: Faber & Faber, 1948)
SC	*Sun Circle* (Edinburgh: Porpoise Press, 1933)
SD	*The Silver Darlings* (London: Faber & Faber, 1941)
SH	*The Shadow* (London: Faber & Faber, 1948)
SL	*Selected Letters* (Edinburgh: Polygon, 1987)
SS	*Second Sight* (London: Faber & Faber, 1940)
WE	*The Well at the World's End* (London: Faber & Faber, 1951)
WGO	*Wild Geese Overhead* (Edinburgh: Chambers, 1991)
YA	*Young Art and Old Hector* (London: Faber & Faber, 1942)

A Note on the Texts

With the exception of *The Serpent* (Canongate Classics, 1997), and *Wild Geese Overhead* (Chambers, 1991), all quotations are from first editions.

Since 1975, all Gunn's novels have been reissued; they continue to move in and out of print. Faber has always retained *The Silver Darlings*, which is usually available. The other publishers concerned are Souvenir Press (London), Canongate Classics (Edinburgh), Richard Drew (Edinburgh), and Polygon (Edinburgh) for *The Atom of Delight*. Richard Drew were acquired by Chambers Harrap and no longer operate as an independent publisher. Canongate aim to keep their Gunn titles in print. These are, at the time of writing, *Highland River, Sun Circle, The Key of the Chest,* and *The Well at the World's End,* as well as *The Serpent.*

1

Life and Background

Born in the year 1891 into a warm and traditional Highland community which during his lifetime was visibly in decline, Neil Miller Gunn lived in the Highlands and drew nourishment from his roots in the Highlands, yet was never merely a 'regional' novelist, never wrote the same book twice, and dealt always with the whole universe of man and the other landscape of the mind.

In 1926, on the evidence of his first novel *The Grey Coast*, C. M. Grieve[1] (Hugh MacDiarmid) who was the initial driving force of the Scottish literary renaissance, forecast that Gunn would 'take rank as the foremost of living Scottish novelists'; when *Morning Tide* was published in 1931, John Buchan described it as 'one of the most remarkable pieces of literature which in recent years have come out of Scotland'; Kurt Wittig wrote in his seminal study *The Scottish Tradition in Literature* (1958) that 'modern Scottish literature reached its peak in the novels of Neil M. Gunn'; and the American Francis Russell Hart[2] devotes more space to Gunn in *The Scottish Novel* than to any other writer. Since Gunn's death in 1973 all his novels have been reissued, a biography, selected letters, collections of his essays and short stories, three book-length critical studies and numerous articles have been published, and no history of Scottish literature could be written without close attention being paid to his work.

Nevertheless, both the *Chambers Biographical Dictionary* and the *Cambridge Biographical Encyclopaedia* still conclude their account of Gunn with the sentence: 'Gunn was at his best when describing the ordinary life and background of a Highland crofting community and when he interprets in simple prose the complex character of the Celt.' This is an oddly patronizing summary of a novelist of European stature who

1

combines intellectual perception and emotional intensity to a remarkable degree, and whose themes deal with the most significant issues of his day.

So what sort of a writer was he? The books can be seen at the same time as an exploration of the history and values of a particular people in a fast-changing predatory world, and as his personal journey from shame and anger at the acid taste of this history, through reassessment of the values themselves, and on into realization that they are fundamental in human nature. Gunn can write with a lucidity as refreshing as spring water, yet his early novels tremble on the edge of passionate obscurity. In several of his books – for example *Highland River*, *The Green Isle of the Great Deep*, and *Bloodhunt* – the prose is clear and strong, the poetic images so natural and immediate as to enter the mind unnoticed, yet each deals with a profound and universal theme – a journey to the source of natural and spiritual life; the tyranny of the analytic intellect applied without moral wisdom; and breaking the vicious circle of violence and revenge.

Gunn conducts his investigations through story, and always claimed to subordinate description, commentary and reflection to the tale itself. This claim may prove difficult to maintain when we examine the books in detail. Gunn disliked rereading them after publication and might have been surprised had he done so to discover the amount of authorial commentary concealed in the text.

In 1960 he wrote to Francis Russell Hart about *The Serpent* (1943),

> You see, I never worked out the moves ahead in a book. In this case I probably got the character going in a first paragraph, and then simply went on, for I never had any difficulty with invention; I was 'told', if you can follow. And often the telling astonished me. If I had known exactly what was going to happen in a book of mine from the beginning I think I would have been too bored to write it. There would have been no surprises on the way. (*SL* 223)

Such an intuitive method is a strength when adrenalin and imagination run together, but a weakness when incidents previously employed in other books slip in to fill a gap in the narrative. Unless a theme, an aim, and a sense of the necessary movement towards fulfilling them are in the mind from the start, no effective story can be told. Gunn knew what he was doing, where he was going, and always told a story.

This is demonstrated when he goes on to Hart:

Sometimes I was bothered a bit about these insights, because I had a liking for them ... but the internal thing that did the 'telling' would stand no nonsense. It kept a continuous rein as it were on my *way*wardness, in the interest of what I could see it believed in as balance.

Gunn started writing comparatively late, publishing his first novel in 1926, at the age of 35. In his early years the only Highland writers of note were the pseudonymous Fiona Macleod (1855–1905), heavily influenced by early Yeats and the Irish 'Celtic Twilight' movement, and the novelist Neil Munro (1864–1930), whose ironic, elegiac tone gave the impression of a latter-day Stevenson troubled by melancholy.

Gunn's youthful struggles with the temptations of Fiona Macleod's silver-grey mysticism, and with the economic decline of the Highlands, made him determined to deal with the real world in front of his eyes, while retaining a deep pride in the ancient Gaelic culture, at that time threatened with extinction.

By the time he began writing seriously, he was fully aware of the poet Hugh MacDiarmid's campaign both to revive the Scots language and to propel Scottish literature into a modernist renaissance, and aware, too, of the new wave of writing in English with which MacDiarmid identified himself – James Joyce, Ezra Pound, T. S. Eliot and the rest.

Gunn later became friendly with both MacDiarmid and Eliot, who was by then a director of Faber & Faber; Gunn's wife Daisy was known to astonish late-talking friends by reciting from 'Rhapsody on a Windy Night': 'Mount./ The bed is open; the toothbrush hangs on the wall,/ Put your shoes at the door, sleep, prepare for life.'

Gunn always had a good word to say for Joyce, not only because Joyce was a writer of astonishing verbal dexterity, but because he felt a strong affinity with Irishness; yet in truth he preferred *Dubliners* to *Ulysses* and viewed *Finnegans Wake* with good-humoured awe; to his mind literature's aim is to communicate. Lawrence he appreciated for the magical empathy of poems like 'Snake', and, in novels, for pages of vivid emotional and descriptive power, but he retreated from those passages in which the author takes the reader by the lapels and shakes him to and fro. Gunn, then, remained his own man, and was no one's disciple.

Neil Gunn was born in Caithness, the austere and windy north-eastern corner of Scotland. He saw himself as a Celtic Highlander – by half-humorous pretence a Pict – but the name Gunn is of Norse origin and he knew very well that his ancestry was mixed.

He grew up in Dunbeath – a Gaelic name – his father the well-respected skipper of a fishing-boat, and his mother a quiet, capable and determined woman with a deep respect for education, who intended her sons to get on in the world. She set her mind against them following their father to sea.

Neil was the seventh of nine surviving children. Only Ben of the seven brothers worked at the fishing before emigrating to Canada, where the two older ones had established themselves. All three returned home to join the Army on the outbreak of the First World War. Two died in France, and the third later of war wounds.

One of the central incidents in the novel *Morning Tide* (1931) is based on the experiences of his younger brother John, but the feelings described are Neil's own. The book shows the boy as a contributing member of a family with its own place in the working community, doing the chores of a croft, running errands, involved unwillingly in the intrigues of his sisters, fighting at school, and escaping whenever possible to run in the open air beyond the reach of even the friendliest eye.

This escape was not a rejection of the rich complexities of family life – he admired his father, loved his mother, and was always so desperate to join older brothers in their forbidden adventures that he had to be chased off with dire threats – but a delight in freedom itself as he let his feet carry him among the scattered rocks, trees and tumbling waters of a natural world which wasn't so much friendly as vividly alive. He was alert to every sound, scent and movement and to those moments of golden stillness out of the wind. It was always necessary for Gunn to preserve that inner self which he discovered when alone, and no one must be allowed to penetrate too deeply.

This was particularly the case at school. He writes in his elusive autobiography *The Atom of Delight* (1956):

4

At school one had to be wary, it was so easy to be touched. Even the most stolid could be dumb in a cunning way, but so long as there was no knowing assault on the inner citadel, rages and thrashings could be borne, like rites in some mysterious initiation which all had to go through on the way to adult freedom. Even irony and sarcasm, those knowing weapons, could be countered by a smouldering rage and hatred, which drew the circle toughly tight. (AD 125)

Luckily, he was a scholar good enough at English and mathematics to escape the worst of the teacher's tantrums, as well as a fighter in emergency, and best of all a swift and elusive runner.

The illumination which came in the fullness of a natural solitude is described vividly in *The Atom of Delight*. The boy is sitting on a boulder in the stream:

The shallow river flowed around and past with its variety of lulling monotonous sounds; a soft wind, warmed by the sun, came upstream and murmured in my ears as it continuously slipped from my face . . .

Then the next thing happened, and happened, so far as I can remember, for the first time. I have tried hard but can find no simpler way of expressing what happened than by saying: I came upon myself sitting there.

Within the mood of content, as I have tried to recreate it, was this self and the self was me.

The state of content deepened wonderfully and everything around was embraced in it.

There was no 'losing' of the self in the sense that there was a blank from which I awoke or came to. The self may have thinned away – it did – but so delightfully that it also remained at the centre in a continuous and perfectly natural way. And then within this amplitude the self as it were became aware of seeing itself, not as an 'I' or an 'ego' but rather as a stranger it had come upon and was even a little shy of. (AD 29–30)

Of course the boy did not then reflect on the experience, and this later account inevitably colours the discovery of what he later came to describe as 'the second self'. But the awakening into a sense of freedom and delight was recalled in adulthood as the revelation of a fundamental psychic reality: 'Here is everything, alive in its own place, and here am I in it!'

In later years when the impulse to go 'off and away' came upon him, he and Daisy drove into the wilds of the West

5

Highlands, sleeping in the car on seats specially adapted to form beds, choosing some hidden place miles from houses, people and preoccupations.

Boyhood came to be for him a touchstone for living experience; he could recapture that feeling of awakening life by revisiting these years in his mind – his father, the sea; his mother, the land; his brothers, the introduction to adventure; his sisters, his initiation into the complexities of emotion and society. The secret self stayed alight.

The river that ran through the strath was his adventure ground and solace. Introduction into the dangerous joys of poaching came early, and poaching forays are described again and again in the novels as if they stand as chosen examples of authentic experience. The community in theory frowned on the game, but in fact saw taking an occasional salmon from the river as an ancient right filched from the people by alien laws. This did not lessen the shame if anyone was caught. The rule was: don't get caught.

Gunn's sister Mary, nine years older than himself, had married a doctor and now lived in Galloway, south-west Scotland, an area often known as 'the Southern Highlands' because of the rugged mountain country beyond Glen Trool. As a move in her plan to separate her sons from the sea, Neil's mother arranged with Mary to invite Neil, not yet 13, to stay with her and study for the Civil Service entrance examination. The doctor later moved to Glenelg and for many years Neil took his holidays with them, treating their house as his home.

Neil was provided with a tutor, a writer of verses and essays for the local paper, who read Tennyson to him on the banks of Loch Ken. The boy was embarrassed at the time, and later chose to play down the influence of Tennyson, but brother John insisted that Neil was still inclined to quote Tennyson and Keats well into his 30s. Neil himself preferred to describe his growing prowess at the game of golf; just over the wall from the doctor's garden was a golf course where he practised effectively enough to win a Civil Service tournament some ten years later.

He had as a second mentor the headmaster of the school at St John's Town of Dalry, who took him fishing, taught him Latin and the names of wild flowers, and suggested that churches should be ringed red on the map to warn of danger.

He sat the exam in Edinburgh, passed, and was called to London, where he worked as a clerk in the Post Office Savings Bank. Characteristically, he was reticent about the shock of being pitched among strangers in the sprawling agglomeration of despoiled villages which was the metropolis, where his background, accent and attitude could have made him a target for derision and hostility.

Athletic ability and the companionship of a few boys from Scotland saved him from isolation, but the appearance again and again in the novels and short stories of the returning failure, viewed as a disgrace for the community, shows the anxiety which haunted him over these years.

He went with friends to music halls, played football for a local club, listened to the radical speakers in Hyde Park, read everything from Huxley,[3] Haeckel[4] and Henry George[5] to the aesthetic fine writing of Walter Pater[6] – a dangerous influence for a future novelist.

From 1909 to 1911 he was posted to Edinburgh, where he learned from older and more worldly colleagues a respect for good wine, and how to engage in civilized discussion.

After passing the final Civil Service examination – which astonished him – he found himself an 'unattached' excise officer travelling the Highlands filling in for 'attached' officers away on leave. During this fancy-free period he met the Irish exciseman Maurice Walsh,[7] who remained a close comrade until he returned to Ireland after the setting up of the Free State in 1921. They climbed mountains, fished legally or illegally on lochs and rivers, shared stories and discussed the world and all that's in it.

When the First World War began, Gunn was given special training and stationed at Kinlochleven routeing ships round minefields and collecting information from the skippers. In the summer he camped on the other side of the loch, took a swim before breakfast, then rowed across to work at the office on the pier.

Eventually he was called to the Army. He went to say goodbye to his mother, who asked with bitter calm, 'Haven't we given enough?' Before he could enter training the war was over.

While at Kinlochleven Gunn started writing poems, stories and essays. When Maurice went back to Ireland they challenged

7

each other to write seriously. Maurice's contribution was *The Key Above the Door*, an outdoor romance which had a healthy sale; Gunn's was *The Grey Coast*, which did not. Both were published in 1926. Walsh went on to become a successful popular novelist, who often appealed to Neil for help with plots.

In 1921 Gunn was assigned to work in Wigan, Lancashire, and he immediately proposed to Jessie Frew (known as Daisy), daughter of a Dingwall jeweller. They were married in the Wigan Registry Office. A house in a miners' row during industrial conflict and the bitter lock-out of that year was a harsh environment for an inexperienced and anxious Daisy, but she was determined to face anything whatsoever for his sake, and the people of Wigan proved generous and hospitable.

The transfer to Lybster in Caithness after a year should have been a joyful experience, but it was not. While away Neil had kept alive a picture of home as he had left it. But now his father and the fishing were both dead. Boats were rotting on the beach. There were no dealers on the quays, no lively fisher-girls waiting to gut the catch. His mother was unwell. The people were dispirited. Gunn toured the impoverished crofting country on excise business and found the prospects bleak.

In 1923 they left Lybster with relief. Gunn had been appointed 'officer attached' to the Glen Mhor distillery in Inverness. They had a bungalow built and as time went by it became a centre for political and literary discussion. Gunn grew active in nationalist agitation, writing articles for newspapers on the economic problems of the Highlands, and every kind of material for the newly established *Scots Magazine*. After publication of the *The Grey Coast* he was regarded as a leading figure in the movement which the poet Hugh MacDiarmid insisted would become the Scottish literary renaissance. In 1929 he joined the newly formed National Party of Scotland and was instrumental, through his contacts and his skill in persuasion, in bringing together the National Party and the more conservative Scottish Party to form the Scottish National Party. His political stance is worth clarifying here, since it has been misinterpreted. Although at one time or another he described himself as a socialist, and then a nationalist, his fundamental views were a good deal more complex than these labels will cover. Gunn distrusted centralized power and the dominance of the State, regarding freedom of expression as the precondition for self-discovery. He wrote to Margaret MacEwen: 'so far as politics are concerned, I am consistently haunted by the hard Scots feeling that they should be kept in their place, their real concern being the providing of the animal necessities of food, shelter and clothing. After that, three cheers for the intensest form of individualism' (*SL* 58).

He looked for practical solutions to real problems through cooperative effort at all levels, writing approvingly of Secretary of State Tom Johnston's[8] view that 'on nine out of ten things for the good of their country all Scots are agreed, but over the tenth they will cut each other's throats, therefore let us forget the tenth and come together on the nine.'

When war began in 1939 the SNP split over support for the war effort. Gunn made his position clear in a letter to SNP secretary John McCormick:[9]

> The forces of the world seem slowly to be aligning themselves into two groups: those who wish to retain man's freedom to express whatever integrity may be in him and those who don't. This freedom of expression is to me supremely important and I am prepared to align myself and fight accordingly... On this issue I am prepared to take a stand for or against any country, my own included (*SL* 60)

As far as philosophical fundamentals are concerned, he wrote to Margaret MacEwen, 'I was always an anarchist,' and again, 'I am... reading a little on anarchism, which I have always found so attractive and which more than once made my concern for the Spanish problem very acute. How I would like to see a country like Spain attempt to put anarchism[10] into practice...' (*SL* 58).

Morning Tide was a commercial and critical success in 1931, and gave Gunn the belief that writing was indeed his life's work. But it may have been in the following year that an unexplained accident caused Daisy to miscarry. The loss of a son haunted Neil all his life. During his last days, when his mind was no longer under control, he talked wildly about the incident, blaming himself. The event caused an estrangement, and probably as a result an intimate relationship began with Margaret MacEwen, younger daughter of Sir Alexander MacEwen, a founder of the Scottish Party and for some years provost of Inverness.

9

The novels which followed *Morning Tide* were not financially successful and in 1935 Frank Morley and T. S. Eliot of Faber and Faber visited Inverness to discuss the future. The result was *Highland River*, which won the James Tait Black Prize in 1937 and was swiftly reprinted. This unexpected triumph persuaded Gunn to leave the excise service and launch himself on a writing career.

He asked Daisy – who was terrified of the idea – to accompany him in a motor boat along the West Coast and round the Isles, a trip recounted in *Off in a Boat* (1938). This was a time of reconciliation in the marriage, which grew deeper, more relaxed and intimate with each year that passed.

The war came as a black cloud so soon after the bold decision to leave the Civil Service that Gunn feared disaster. But, despite paper shortage and production problems, not only were books more widely read during the war than at any previous time, but three of Gunn's best novels were issued and highly successful – *The Silver Darlings* (1941), *The Serpent* (1943) and *The Green Isle of the Great Deep* (1944). He also wrote regular notes on the countryside in wartime for the *Scots Magazine*, pieces designed to hearten readers and relieve the almost intolerable tensions of daily life. They were eventually published in book form as *Highland Pack* (1949), together with articles originally written for *Chambers' Journal*.

After the war Gunn's books became more experimental and less profitable. The enthusiasm of his publishers waned. It is true that some of them are flawed as novels but it is often in the flawed books that we find the most penetrating insights. After the autobiographical *Atom of Delight* (1956), which for some Scottish writers has proved an inspirational text, he gave up writing except in answer to specific requests for articles or essays. But he was not idle. He served on the commission which investigated the health and future of crofting, and the Commission which looked into the state of Scottish hospitals, acted as consultant to a distilling company, and gave patient and practical advice to a number of younger writers as well as delivering radio talks and participating in discussion programmes for the BBC.

In 1963 his wife Daisy died. Their companionship had grown so close in the previous twenty-five years that Gunn wrote in a letter, 'I'd destroy all I ever made for one glimpse of her sitting out on the patio in front of me, weeding.' Daisy was shy with strangers, and spoke little in company, but was sure of her own perceptions and had a gleaming gaiety which shone through among friends.

Left alone, Gunn concentrated on the achievement of inner clarity, despite various debilitating medical conditions. He disliked the negative tone of contemporary literature. He wrote, 'I cannot find an instance where... "negative emotions" do not lead to sterility and destruction. If literature exists only to tell about them...there ain't no point in writing at all.' This is a far cry from the negative emotions which overwhelm *The Grey Coast* and *The Lost Glen*. Towards the end of his life he remarked, 'Perhaps all literature does is to give you a few friends.'

Gunn was a warm, wise and courteous man with a manner which can best be described as objective friendliness. He developed over the years a remarkable patience with the unpleasant manifestations of others. His reticence in personal matters was tied so closely with courtesy and pride that the pride might well be missed by the casual observer. His gift for friendship and his pleasure in congenial company were legendary. He found his greatest joy in the comradeship of shared ploys or in conversation which undertook an intellectual or spiritual quest. At any time one of his verbal arabesques could lead him into that region of light where humour is the natural catalyst and conversation would dissolve in laughter.

Neil Gunn died in 1973. Before turning attention to the books, let me quote his own advice: 'One only does anything by doing a bit at a time – because far in is the inner light that sees, and that you know is there, and has meaning, and is our only glimpse of truth.'

2

The Fruits of Bitterness:
The Grey Coast and *The Lost Glen*

When Gunn's first novel, *The Grey Coast*, appeared in 1926 from Jonathan Cape, it was praised, by those who chose to notice the book, mainly for its 'realism'.

The first few paragraphs show clearly enough that realism was indeed the initial intention of the writer:

> Before she called her uncle to tea, she had drawn the cheap slip of window-curtain to one side, so that the last of the daylight might be made use of and paraffin saved. Now as her uncle pushed back his plate and cup, and sucked at a tooth, and cleared his throat, saying 'Ha!' and 'Huhuh!' in husky, replete grunts, she observed through the darkening a figure enter by the slap in the dyke at the foot of the potato patch. Her features stiffened perceptibly.
>
> But her uncle's quick, crafty eyes did not fail to catch that look, that stiffening expression, and twisting his wizened neck he peered blinkingly through the window.
>
> 'Is that someone coming, Maggie?'
>
> 'Ay,' she said laconically, for his long vision was as good as her own. (*GC* 7)

These few sentences are rich in information, the subtlety concealed by clarity of diction, as if such directness must be without guile. But it isn't. Without the need for description or explanation we sense the claustrophobic atmosphere of the household. We know without being told that there is no openness between the old man and the young girl. Each attempts to conceal from the other both intentions and reactions to events. Maggie is reticent, Jeems is sly. Their knowledge of the other's stratagems is acute but never put into words. On Maggie's part, this is a defensive ploy. On the part of Uncle

Jeems, deviousness, secrecy and manipulation give him what satisfaction he can extract from his declining years.

We learn, too, that they live close to poverty – the cheap slip of curtain, the need to save paraffin; we sense Maggie's concealed revulsion at her uncle's deliberate uncouthness; we know that she recognizes the visitor, who is unwelcome, and that Jeems knows this, and relishes it.

We gather subliminally that they receive few visitors, but this one is only too regular a tapper on the door; and more than that, we read between the lines Maggie's fear of being caught in a trap from which she cannot escape. Altogether it is a passage of considerable accomplishment.

The movement of the book is slow and confined in time and space. Maggie lives with her uncle Jeems because she has nowhere else to go, acting as housekeeper and helping on the croft. Jeems occupies himself with poaching and counting the money he has hidden under the floorboards of an outhouse. He delights in exploiting the prosperous neighbour who is known by the name of his farm as 'Tullach', drawing from him every kind of help by dangling the bait of Maggie as a future wife.

The bully Tullach bides his time. He wants Maggie carnally more intensely each day, and humours Jeems to get her, but Jeems spins out the waiting in order to gather from Tullach every last drop of gain.

Tullach strides about in satisfaction that 'what he was doing he was doing solidly, with the dignity of a man of substance, and the end was inevitable'. The 'end', of course, is Maggie. But his mind grows jumpy, and his body impatient.

Eventually Tullach tries brutally to force Maggie, and fails – a scene replicated in more intensely charged language by the Colonel's assault on Mary Mackinnon in *The Lost Glen*:

> Gradually all his body began to come at her. She did not break away or shout wildly. Her flesh froze, her lips and face narrowed in a cold deadliness. Suddenly he enveloped her, snatched her bodily with a fierce grunt, so that the milk-pail splashed against his leg; crushed her, crushed her, as though each constriction were a gluttonous oath... (GC 269)

Maggie's mind is centred on the young fisherman Ivor, and his on her, yet they will not confess their feelings, and even find

13

difficulty in exchanging words when they meet. Ivor feels himself condemned to useless poverty in a community where fishing is dead and no alternative exists. Defeated by his negative irony Maggie cannot make the first move.

When Gunn writes of Ivor's state of bitter depression, the language either grows overcharged to the point of obscurity or is in danger of flying away with the pseudo-Celtic poetry of Fiona Macleod. This was the pseudonym of William Sharp, born in Paisley and in his prime a London journalist, who adopted the persona of a Celtic 'wise-woman' and proclaimed the Celts to be a doomed race, with much use of the words 'grey', 'shadow', 'wings' and 'white light'.

In *The Grey Coast* Gunn sets out to present Caithness as a region with its industry gone and its people under a spiritual cloud, but at the same time to repudiate Fiona. Yet his own tone is at once angry and fatalistic, while Fiona's 'grey' proves to be a dominant word throughout the book.

Indeed, Maggie sees everything in shades of grey:

> The whole croft was mean. Life was mean, mean and bare, with no colour to it, no warmth, nothing but the eternal greyness, that was a poverty, an exhaustion as of an animal hunger, gnawing at stones for bread.

The landscape itself is subjected to ironic overkill through Ivor's eyes:

> cliffs flawed as in a half-sardonic humour of their Creator to permit of the fishing-creek, was surely the place for the perfect growth of this duality of the mind, whereby the colourless, normal life becomes at once a record of the stolidly obvious and of the dream-like unknown. (*GC* 14).

This intellectual extravagance destroys the refreshing directness with which the story began. We continually meet descriptions of the land and coast which register not as objective realism but as expressions of the author's own bitterness standing behind Ivor and driving him on. Caithness is seen as 'a land of knotted rheumatism and dead things'; we hear of 'the everlasting grey vagueness of the croft and of the coast'.

Ivor, like Ewan in the succeeding novel *The Lost Glen*, is in a state of self-blighting negativity, described as 'the grey mist of soul-weariness. An utter weariness of self, a self-mockery.' He is

14

convinced that he cannot offer marriage to Maggie since he has no prospects for a livelihood. When he tries to get close to her he fails: 'Yet he could not break through and touch her; he could not – he could not; every muscle was netted, in his perversity, his emotion was netted and strangled. He could not break through to take her in his arms, to crush her.' (GC 27).

The repetition of phrases and the need to 'crush her' reveal the current of violence and sexual tension which runs through the book.

The encounter between Ivor and the schoolmaster Moffatt brings Fiona Macleod back from the dead. Moffatt tries to extract from Ivor some comment on the Celtic literary movement by reading aloud Yeats's 'Lake Isle of Innisfree'. Ivor's only comment is, 'Sounds nice.' Eventually Moffatt cries out impatiently to the studiously indifferent Ivor that surely literature must relate directly to life or it's useless? Ivor says, 'Ay.'

When Ivor has gone, Moffatt is left wondering 'what the devil was really in his mind all the time?' He lifts a volume of Fiona Macleod, throws it aside, and recites from 'Innisfree' 'Peace comes dropping slow... midnight's all a glimmer, and noon a purple glow... full of the linnet's wings.'

Moffatt is enacting Gunn's own early struggle against Fiona Macleod and all that Sharp's elevated alter ego stood for. The attitude remains ambiguous, as if he is tempted to wonder 'are we really like that, after all?' It is a bitter struggle because throughout his life as a novelist we can see Gunn striving to unite an account of life as it is lived with the metaphysical dimension of meaning. This is a quest which requires the greatest possible honesty of intention. Fiona's illusory mysticism is not the most nourishing food for the journey.

The result is that although Gunn uses *The Grey Coast* as an antidote to Fiona, the overall tone remains one of bitter melancholy and he fails to resolve the living human problem posed in the book.

Having created a unity of atmosphere, character and story, he introduces a sudden happy ending. A twist of plot is allowed to shed an abruptly contradictory light on the whole scene. It is as if a long dour siege has been lifted only by authorial intervention, leaving the reader in a state of arrested doubt.

15

In truth, though, it is not the plot which undermines *The Grey Coast* but the overcharged language in which Ivor is depicted, so that as an individual he disappears into linguistic obscurity. The reason for this, I think, is that the author identifies too closely with the character; a necessary detachment is lost, and a kind of literary self-consciousness creeps in to take its place.

In his second novel, *The Lost Glen*, written in 1926, the year of publication for *The Grey Coast*, he moves even farther from objective realism into the bitter irony of anger and defeat.

The book has an odd history. To Gunn's chagrin it was rejected not only by Cape but by five other London publishers. This was an attack on pride which he could not dismiss. He had believed his literary career to be launched, but now he was knocked back to a pawn's square on the chessboard.

His reaction was to accuse London publishers of bias against a novel which deals with the true state of Scotland, and to persuade the friendly editor of the *Scots Magazine* to publish the book in instalments.

When Hodder and Stoughton returned *The Lost Glen*, Gunn replied indignantly that the book was 'the first honest attempt at introducing the Highlands as they are today'.

Hodder's reply to this acted as a red rag to the bull, when it loftily declared 'that the economic, political and other significance of the decay of Highland life would not have much appeal to the non-Scottish general reader'.

This is the first example of the enduring London view that to write of life in the Highlands makes you strictly a 'regional writer', operating on the distant edge of the civilized world, with nothing of value to say about the human situation in general. By insisting on the specific Highlandness of the book, Gunn in his justified intolerance missed his own point, which is that the value of human beings, their culture and their stratagems for dealing with reality are of fundamental interest wherever they are found, provided the subject is treated with insight, vigour and subtlety.

Forced to put *The Lost Glen* into a drawer, Gunn had an inspiration which enabled him to move away from the doom and gloom of contemporary Caithness into the living community of his boyhood, The book which followed was the saving of his career. *Morning Tide* (1931) became a Book Society Choice and a commercial success for the new Scottish publisher Porpoise Press.

The interim publication of a collection of short stories, *Hidden Doors* (1929), and an excursion into drama, had done nothing for his income or reputation.

Some of the short stories share the overcharged sexuality and extravagant language which characterize *The Lost Glen* – 'she gave him the mystical wine and honey, and she gave him the image of red lips like yielding ripe fruit' – but some are alive with character and memorable directness: 'on the windy uprise of the croft Hendry might be seen now and then... niggling at the ground like an overgrown crow. "He's maybe worth his meat," said brother John on one of those rare sardonic moments when he offered an opinion about anything.' Collections of short stories, though, are not popular with bookshops, and Porpoise Press published reluctantly.

The entrance into drama was a serious effort to break new ground. One play, 'The Ancient Fire' was performed at the Lyric, Glasgow in 1929. The experimental attempt to show characters speaking at one time from behind their social mask, at another from the uncensored unconscious, proved to bewilder rather than enlighten the audience.

Morning Tide, on the contrary, was the most commercially successful book issued by the Porpoise Press in its short career, so when Gunn took *The Lost Glen* out of its drawer and asked them to publish, how could they refuse?

George Blake, who now ran the firm with George Malcolm Thomson, ventured a tactful warning about the proposal: 'Whatever you write and publish now is of vast importance. You will be judged stringently by a large and rather jealous public, to whom you certainly owe a duty, and they will not be content with less than your best.'

Gunn dismissed the warning. To him *The Lost Glen* was unfinished business. Its rejection left unsaid something which unappeased emotion demanded should be said. He could not write another book until that demand was satisfied. As he put it later, he had to 'get rid of something'. The public would face the plight of the Highlands whether it wanted to or not.

It is one of the mysteries of fiction writing that in a novel a man private by nature and jealous of his inner integrity can reveal feelings without reserve which pride would refuse to allow in life. All the more humiliating if, in the writing, balance has been lost, and this becomes obvious to the world. In 1961 Gunn pretended not to remember *The Lost Glen* at all, and treated it as if with a pair of tongs, saying 'there is a too-muchness which embarrasses'.

Disillusion and despair about the Highland situation, and with what he perceives to be his people's apathy in face of it, are expressed with a fierce and confused intensity. As time went by this confusion clarified into a fundamental question: Has the culture of the Highlands anything to offer which would justify his own sense of grievance?

All this makes *The Lost Glen* (1932) the most difficult of all Gunn's novels to deal with. The story is inadequate to its theme. When control breaks down, melodrama is the result, and melodrama is a poor argument. Passages of felicitous insight share the page with language so thick with emotion that words grow clogged and dark.

The basic situation is one which reappears with very different effect in *The Key of the Chest* (1945) and *The Drinking Well* (1946): the young man returning home a failure from the south, the humiliation more shameful if disgrace accompanies him, and if the community has financed his education.

Gunn's mother determined that her sons should not follow their father to sea, and Neil went south to make a life for himself. He returned with a safe job as a credit to his family. But the sense of obligation had been a secret burden, as these novels demonstrate.

Like *The Grey Coast*, *The Lost Glen* has a direct and effective first paragraph.

> Ewan Macleod was aware that his disgrace was known before the bus drew up by the small post office a hundred yards short of the hotel. The usual waiting group all looked at the outcast student, the older ones secretively, but the youngsters with a stare. (*LG* 9)

His father greets Ewan with simple sincerity, but 'Eyes, when they could, peered at him with inhuman penetration, for he personated so much in the way of monstrous behaviour.' (*LG* 9).

What horrible crime, then, has he committed? It is one of the weaknesses of the book that the cause of Ewan's disgrace is not strong enough to bear the weight of the story. He was financed at college by his soberly prosperous Uncle William, not from

18

affection but from a dour sense of duty. Ewan is celebrating exam success with fellow students, some of whom are drunk, and all of whom are noisy. As Uncle William unexpectedly enters, a loud argument has begun between a Highland youth and an intellectual Edinburgh snob. Ewan's reserve and unwillingness to apologize for the unseemly behaviour of one and all drive Uncle William in fury from the room, repudiating the scapegrace outright as he goes. Ewan returns home because pride refuses the cowardice of disappearing nowhere.

From this point on, the plot relentlessly stacks the cards against him. Ewan goes to sea with his father when a storm is brewing; the boat capsizes and his father drowns. He is blamed for it. He becomes a gillie for the hotel and regards this menial job as a humiliation. He will not approach Mary Mackinnon, the girl he had hoped to marry, because he believes he could not support her, his mother and two sisters.

The situation is made more disturbing by a sense that the author identifies too closely with Ewan, as if there were some confusion in his mind between self-pride and inner integrity. When we are told of Ewan's 'desire not to touch the reality of life in his native place' we feel in the writer a personal revulsion against the passivity of his people. He is forcing himself to deal with a situation which he finds intolerable. The expression of Ewan's mood is often violent: 'We're living on a dead past like ravens on a dead sheep. When the sheep is completely rotten we too shall pass.'

The drama centres on Ewan's growing hatred for the bullying Colonel Hicks, a permanent resident at the hotel, whose assumption of superiority and dominance makes him the embodiment of all the forces which have destroyed the Highland way of life and demeaned its culture. It is said: 'the Colonel and himself were chance figures in a drama that affected the very earth under his feet...as if they stood for an ultimate conquest or defeat' (LG 110).

The Colonel is not a protagonist worthy of being raised to such a cosmic level, and by the end is seen with sudden clairvoyance by his niece as a lost and pathetic outcast. The author is pumping up the Colonel to justify the emotional capital invested in the book.

To justify the inflated language a tragic ending becomes

19

inevitable. Despite this investment in the Colonel, the encounters to which the most attention is given are those between Ewan and Clare, the Colonel's English niece, in the Highlands to recuperate from an illness. Ewan is appointed by the hotel as her gillie and the relationship slides step by step towards the sexual.

Clare emerges as a character with genuine honesty and intelligence who finds herself in an impossible situation from which she does not even want to break free. Ewan's reactions, on the other hand, seem dark and perverse. He feels 'not so much a fine rapture as a fine torment. And therefore none the less fascinating.'

After each passionate encounter he withdraws into irony. Gunn knew well enough that irony is a form of self-protection, which can eventually destroy the capacity to see everything afresh. At one point Ewan refers to 'a slip into this painful self-consciousness which is a part of pride'. The moods of *The Lost Glen* swing from celebration of pride, through self-knowledge to defeatism.

One narrative climax comes almost accidentally when the Colonel finds Mary Mackinnon alone and is taken with a fit of desire mixed with cruelty and contempt. The language combines over-excitement with a peculiar sexual disgust:

> All the animal scents of the byre assailed his nostrils, the infesting smell of dung, of secretive bodily acts. Lust itself became the incense of dominance... His body surged up in a harmony of power.

He begins 'gibbering in a fierce incoherence' (*LG* 250). We are dangerously close to caricature.

The melodramatic ending when Ewan – again almost accidentally – encounters the Colonel is itself ironic. Ewan is determined to destroy the man because he imagines, wrongly, that Hicks has made Ewan's sister Jean pregnant. This almost meaningless tragedy is a declaration of despair not only from Ewan himself but from the story-teller, who has apparently abandoned control.

A dual death solves nothing, and makes an entirely negative statement. It must seem to Mary and her father a betrayal and desertion; it will crush his mother's already fragile will to live; it will blight the lives of his sisters Jean and Annabel; and for Clare must bring a sense of revulsion against everything she experienced in the Highlands.

The title *The Lost Glen* is not accidental; it is a pity that the story it refers to is not more deeply embedded in the novel's texture. Basic to the intention, but never realized, is a view of the Highlands as a legendary paradise despoiled. When the piper Colin Mackinnon, Mary's father, was 18 years old, he lost his way in the hills, lay down in darkness and at last fell into a sleep of exhaustion. He woke with the sun shining on a glen which he knew with uncanny certainty had never before been visited by a human being.

This vision of the lost glen stayed with Colin for the rest of his life, and from time to time brought into his mind scraps of a pipe tune which had 'the sweet fresh feeling of a first morning in creation'. One day, at a moment of crisis in his life, when his mother was ill and he felt himself at the end of his strength, the melody in its entirety formed itself in his head. With a feeling of liberation from long captivity he played it through. When he got home his mother was on the way to recovery.

This notion of a Golden Age had been close to Gunn's heart as a young man. His friend, the painter Keith Henderson, would argue fiercely with him, demanding a date for the Golden Age, and insisting that unless he could pin it down in time then he must abandon the idea as delusion. Gunn was unmoved.

The overall effect of the book makes the inner story of the pipe tune invisible. *The Lost Glen* received adverse criticism which affected Gunn deeply at a time when he was peculiarly vulnerable. My suspicion is that the cause of the anguish was not the criticism itself but an inner knowledge that the criticism was justified. Deep down he was aware of the 'too muchness' of which he later accused himself.

3

Rescue: *Morning Tide*

The decision to recreate the fresh vision and sensitivities of boyhood rescued Gunn from violent bitterness. He had a deep need to discover whether anything permanent exists in the psyche, whether integrity is possible in the face of repeated assaults on pride and self-respect. If it does exist, it must be present from the start. It must be fundamental, an essence.

To return to his early life in Dunbeath would bring back the reality of light. The material was so familiar that there would be no room for doubt.

Between the years 1891 and 1903 when he was growing up in Caithness, the economy was already threatened, but fishing still granted a livelihood to his father, and the whole community retained a pattern to include all generations. A boy could run, jump and fall with a sense of security.

The story explores moments of stress, crisis, adventure and celebration within an integrated family. Hugh is a reluctant witness to the growing sexual rivalry of his sisters; he loves and escapes from his mother, who hates the sea; he helps and admires his father, but at a distance; he follows brother Alan when allowed; he fights enemies at school and falls out with friends; he watches his father save their boat in a storm. Above all, he runs through the living texture of the world and into loneliness as at once a refuge and a positive joy.

Hugh is the eye of the story. Only occasionally do we share the thoughts and feelings of sister Kirsty or sister Grace. We are involved with Hugh at an intimate, nervous level, yet the story has its own life.

The book begins with Hugh gathering mussels at ebb-tide on the shore. His father has hooks to bait.

Below the high-tidal sweep of tangleweed the beach sloped in clean grey-blue stones rounded and smooth, some no bigger than his fist, but some larger than his head. As he stepped on them they slithered and rolled with a sea-noise. The noise rose up and roared upon the dark like a wave... It was too lonely a place to make a noise. (*MT* 8)

We are alone there, and boy-size already.

The boy lifted his dark head and looked about the boulders as though his thought might have been overheard. There was an uncertain, defensive smile on his face, which faded immediately he was sure he was alone. His hands were now bitterly cold. He could not feel his fingers. (*MT* 10)

This is deep into Gunn country – simultaneously inside the boy and watching him, self-conscious yet acutely aware of the world around him.

Hugh's sense that his aloneness, his privacy, may be penetrated, causes him nervous anguish throughout the book. His sisters are dangerous – Kirsty may sympathize her way in, or Grace charm her way in. Hugh has a dozen stratagems to protect his secret self, and stratagems to deal with his own feelings. When the cold grows so savage that it brings tears to his eyes 'he would not cry. He only pretended to cry in order to ease the anguish.' (*MT* 11).

He has, too, an acute awareness of something evasive in the nature of the world, which always moves just out of sight:

The loneliness of the bouldered beach suddenly caught him in an odd way. A small shiver went over his back. The dark undulating water rose from him to a horizon so far away that it was vague and lost: it could heave up and drown the whole world. (*MT* 13)

Sensitivity extends to natural life: 'The wind started sniffing here and there like a treacherous dog'; and even to the behaviour of boats: 'the boat went languid, her head fell off; with a weak sidelong gesture she disappeared down the wave's back'; 'As his body stood fixed, space crept all round it'. The secret of this writing is a vital detachment.

There are glimpses, too, of another dimension. 'Her mother did not answer. She was standing quite still and listening. Grace began to listen too; and it was as though by listening they brought the demon of the storm within the kitchen' (*MT* 68); 'a grey haar coming off the water like a ghost's breath'. As Hugh stands in the ancient broch above the village, 'A person was alone here, was cut off from the living world. Yet this ancient world was anything but dead. Even the stones were too quiet for that, too knowing. ' (*MT* 211–12).

Kirsty, we are told, 'had the rare quality that is called imagination and her eyes had often to remain steady in order to let her imagination go to work' (*MT* 48). When her mother is ill, her life in danger, Kirsty's voice becomes the voice of a seer, alarming Hugh:

> 'You know, away in the time of the Preacher and in these strange places, mother would be a woman among them, wise and calm, smiling and hospitable and welcoming them. Our mother. She would. In some ways the world here is little ... And these wifies who go moaning about their religion – they don't understand mother, they don't see the greatness of her spirit.' (*MT* 279)

Some critics are suspicious of Gunn's tendency to see people as archetypes – the Mother, the Father, the Boy – quoting in evidence such comments as 'He was being born to the earth that is behind all mothers, as the sea, the father, is behind all fathers.' I take no exception to this. The human race goes back a long way. Without fathers and mothers it wouldn't exist. We don't need 'a race memory' to recognize that. Certainly a novel in which the characters were not individuals but symbols would grow tiresome. This does not happen. Hugh's mother and father are alive in a living community, acting with their own singularity. Kirsty is fully entitled to her view.

At one point it is said: 'The mother passed the cups of tea. She had the natural air of dispensing life's mercies. Her movements were soothing and sufficient. She was the starting point of a circle that finished in her.' (*MT* 44). Just so. My own mother was the same.

The most moving scene in *Morning Tide* (1931) is that in which elder brother Alan leaves for Australia, unable to face going to sea in opposition to his mother's wishes. His father would like nothing better than to have at least one son with him, to give continuity to the life he has built up, but has too much respect for his wife to speak. Alan's mother would rather know her son to be alive in Australia, unseen on the other side of the world, than to lie awake on a night of storm with husband and son at the mercy of the sea.

'Goodbye, Mother,' said Alan, 'goodbye.'
'Goodbye, Alan,' said his mother.

Then Alan, still shaking his mother's hand, unable to let it go, 'strongly put his left hand round her shoulders, drew her to him, and kissed the first part of her head that met his mouth'.

At that all her supreme courage completely left her. In a moment from being calm and self-possessed, she was sobbing in a way that shook all her body. Her face was hidden, her shoulders heaved, her sobs were harsh racking sounds.

... He had no memory of having ever kissed his mother before or of having been kissed by her. When she drew back and looked at him, her eyes were clairvoyant and terrible through their glistening tears. He followed the others, still murmuring, 'Never mind, Mother!' (*MT* 195)

Most of the village is there to see them off. Their farewell is cheerful. But as the men leave, 'their smiles were weary, as though there was a final element in them of defeat. The grass had grown greyer, the trees barer. Virtue had been drained out of the place, out of themselves.'(*MT* 204).

We are back with the situation of *The Lost Glen* but now the narrative has control.

Not long after this the mother falls ill. She must live with the fact that she has driven her son out of the community, and in so doing hurt her husband's pride in his family and in his livelihood. She never speaks of it.

Pride with the men is a potent force. Alan's pride ensures that he is merry as the bus leaves for the south. His father's pride ensures that he speaks calmly and positively to his neighbours as his hope for the future vanishes round a bend in the road.

In Gunn's work secrecy is the necessary accompaniment to pride. After watching his father bring in his boat, Hugh's 'pride could afford to become immoderate because he repressed it for pride's sake'. When Hugh emerges from the ruined broch in which he has been beset by fears, 'when you could do all this alone, you got a certain secret power. It remained hidden in you, a live strength.' (*MT* 212). The impression given is that loneliness is Hugh's preferred state, and secrecy a positive quality, a method of storing power.

Despite Grace's betrayal of her sister, Alan's departure, and his mother's illness, Hugh's adventures present us with a positive response to experience, and celebrate the resilience and creative light in human beings, and their ability to bring alive a functioning community. The book ends, 'His head turned. And all at once he started running, his body light and fleet, his bare legs twinkling across the fields of the dawn.' When Hugh sets off running it is not to deny the community in which he lives, but to celebrate freedom. *Morning Tide* embodies both.

4

The Way Through History

SUN CIRCLE

It would seem sensible to consider the three historical novels together, although they were neither written nor published consecutively. To do so may give a clearer picture of the overall achievement they represent.

Sun Circle, first issued in 1933, is a violent, richly textured story, thick with the same sexual tension which characterizes *The Lost Glen*. But it is a great deal more than that. Through a harsh, intense account of invasion, betrayal and defeat, Gunn struggles with problems he could face only by placing them in a remote and secret time, in the 'privacy' of historical fiction.

The book delves down into the psychological roots of evil and violence, and embodies also a hypersensitive examination of the temptations to cruelty which one form of intellectual/aesthetic detachment can bring. Aniel, favoured disciple of the unnamed Druidic Master, can be seen as in this sense a bitterly acute version of a characteristic Gunn sees in himself.

The novel becomes in the end an effort to establish in his own mind the continuity of values, and through this the significance of human life itself. By means of the Master's teaching, he seeks to create a philosophical and psychological response to fear, hatred and defeat. This involves the invention of a Druidic vision of the world, as well as an examination of the early Christian mission.

The period of Norse raids on the coast of Caithness is so sparsely documented that its wildness, darkness, depth and distance set his imagination alight and set it free.

Columba's conversion of the northern region of what is now Scotland (which probably meant little more than pragmatic adherence to Christianity by a few chiefs and rulers) took place in the sixth century, while Norse raids and eventual occupation of the Orkneys and much of Caithness are generally attributed to the ninth. That is a wide gap, and whether the pagan religion was as enduring, and ever became so refined, as is shown here, and whether the Christian missionary priest would be so isolated there is no means of telling. Gunn read the historical accounts available to him, and imagination must be allowed its own authority. In the story the coast is attacked by Norse reivers who sack, burn, loot, and bear off captives into slavery wherever they land. The folk of the place are, we are told, 'a dark, intricate people, loving music and fun'. The tribes owe loose allegiance to a far off king, but operate in self-contained communities, each under its own chief, who can expect no help from that source.

Alongside the tribe of the Ravens live, secret and elusive in their round houses, the aboriginal 'Finlags', a 'dwarfish race' who speak 'the old language', and are neither to be trusted nor understood, for they move with their own lore in hidden ways, like cunning moles, but more dangerous.

South of the Ravens are the Logenmen, wary to the point of hostility, who take the opportunity of Viking assault to raid the Ravens' cattle. This is one of the many references forward to what Gunn saw as the tragedy of Scottish history – that internal feuding which lets in the external enemy, and makes full cultural development impossible.

As always with Gunn, concern is not simply with physical and psychological conflict, but with the fundamental spiritual currents which move within and work through history. This intense metaphysical preoccupation disconcerts some readers, yet the emotional drive of the tale is so strong that if it is accepted as it runs, spiritual and physical form a unity which burns in the mind, while the intuitive blending of history with thought and legend creates an almost hallucinatory sense of life.

The tribe of the Ravens is nominally Christian. The missionary priest Molrua has established himself among them, under the protection of the Chief's wife Silis. Yet the ancient Grove with its dark trees and standing stones remains peopled by the Master and his pupils. Drust, Chief of the Ravens, accepts his wife's Christianity yet resents her rigorous zeal and assumption of righteousness as a slur on his manhood, at one point bursting out with, 'There would never be peace in this accursed place until she was riding on their backs as they crawled to the Christian priest.' (*SC* 81).

Molrua instructs the people that they cannot serve both God and Mammon, that the rites and sacrifices of the Grove are evil; but their minds move more subtly and deviously than he can guess. To worship both God and Mammon was 'for them not only simple, but wise and needful'. 'There are hidden, evil things and dark spirits whom we must defeat if we are to be Christians...But Molrua does not know what the Master knows.' Again, 'Deep in their marrow, Christ was a make-believe, a white shadow.' Gunn is concerned to hold the balance. The spiritual conflict is not prejudged but held in the mind as a whole. Molrua and the Master each represents his own religion at its purest – Molrua, Christianity at its vital flowering before hierarchy, dogma and discipline distorted the teaching; the Master, the old religion at its most refined, one rising as the other falls on the tide of history.

Drust's wife Silis brings to mind the history of Scottish religious fanaticism as the comment is made, 'for one could so work for the conversion of others that the sway of authority thereby engendered tended to puff up the mind in its lust for power, and God's name was used for terror, and Christ's name as a threat' (*SC* 173–4).

Molrua himself presents the Christian story 'in all its newness and strange and terrible beauty, so strange and beautiful that it had the air about it still of the incredible. And because the incredible was true, the heart rose in surprise and gladness.' (*SC* 92).

Molrua's mind is shown in its simplicity and beauty as he watches the Northmen move about below him:

> Under the morning it was a strange thing to see men so behave...Their limbs and their weapons stirred like the legs of great spiders...Strange to watch their dark antics in the fresh light of so clear a morning. Strange that these creatures should be God's creatures too. (*SC* 172).

Gunn's intuitive artistry makes Molrua's death a symbol and legend of Christianity's infection blowing on the winds of history.

A raider kills him in the act of blessing, and ransacks his hut in search of loot. There is nothing there of value except the bound copy of the Gospels.

> At the door again, the Northman glanced about him, glanced at the vellum pages of the scriptures in his hands and threw them from him. It was altogether a queer place this, and quite possibly he had killed one of the terrible magicians who offered up sacrifices with black rites.
>
> He strode away, but at the crest had to look over his shoulder. There was no one there, nothing but the dead body and a leaf of that which he had thrown from him moving in the wind. (*SC* 179)

The Master makes few appearances, but each appearance is of profound significance in the story. Whatever may be said of the historical accuracy of the Master's teaching, it is authentic to Gunn's perceptions in the year 1933 of a way through the terrors and humiliations of the world. The Master's achievement is to have reached 'the dividing of forces with no gain and no loss, and no question of reward except the reward of being there; therefore may we feel that it possesses human loneliness in its naked form' (*SC* 117).

This acceptance of, and even relish for, loneliness, permeates the whole book. The Master claims 'in the final loneliness we have faced the malignant cruelty that is part of all Beyond; facing that, we have caught the balanced moment of all-seeing that is our moment of serenity' (*SC* 116).

There is an echo here of Gunn's schoolboy drawing the circle 'toughly tight', but not of the joyful serenity of the boy in the stream. Cruelty seen as an eternal reality in the nature of the 'Beyond' remains one of Gunn's fundamental insights, despite his later emphasis on 'wonder' and 'delight'; indeed it becomes the subject of his last and most intensely metaphysical novel, *The Other Landscape*.

Loneliness is a constant theme for young Aniel too, whose moods veer and plunge through tenderness, lust, cruelty, playfulness and a dark need for dominance and control, but who retains always the ability to watch both himself and others. He teases and seduces the dark, wild and erratic Breeta, tormenting and entrapping her with endearing wiles and sudden violence. 'Aniel chattered, netting her, drawing her deeper within the conspiracy.' They engage in furious coupling beside the corpse of the Northman Aniel has killed from behind.

Yet it is continually emphasized that 'in his drawing and carving he had known the loneliness of delight...There had been a secrecy about that, stirring the emotions,' and 'There came at times an odd quality of detachment to Aniel's emotions; it was the mind working behind the emotions.'(SC 207). In moods of revulsion 'He was glad to be rid of her [Breeta], glad to be rid of them all, glad to be rid of the Master, glad to be alone.' (SC 310). At the worst, his mind dwells in a cold, edged malice, 'his mind taut with its own malevolence, his sight swift and smiling' (SC 311). Only at the end does he find himself 'staring at the bleached horror of loneliness' (SC 312).

It is one of the book's problems that through the teeming spate of characters, violent action and psychological probing, Aniel remains the central figure, and the reader has to deal continually with his veering moods and betrayals. He claims to love and admire the Master but forgets him in pursuit of Breeta. He betrays Breeta in passionate desire for Nessa, the Chief's golden-haired, provocative daughter. And it is Nessa who not only betrays her people with the Northman Haakon, but seeks to lure Aniel into collusion with the betrayal.

The most appalling betrayal is Aniel's own when, hypnotized by the expectations of the defeated and desperate Ravens, he leads Breeta towards sacrifice as a victim to appease the dark gods; his integrity is saved only by the intervention of the Master and the assault of fire which devours the sacred Grove.

Aniel's cat-and-mouse play with the dark and darting Breeta shows a detachment close to cruelty, the emotion which in later books Gunn consistently and analytically condemned. The Master's teaching required detachment, but as an aid to understanding, and with no taint of cruelty or malevolence, and he sees clean through Aniel's physical and intellectual lusts and tells him: The teaching is perfectly simple: see clearly. No one can see clearly if malevolence infects the vision.

Gunn was asking the question: is wisdom possible for an artist of Aniel's kind – and of Gunn's kind? He writes: 'Aniel was a maker and a maker can retreat from what evil he has done, or from whatever has come upon him, to the happy solitude of his own creation, and yet have a cunning understanding of that evil.' But is this enough?

It is made explicit in *Sun Circle* that those human beings who imagine and create, and those who endure and keep the world alive, are of more value to spiritual survival than the conquering heroes and rulers, for the ruler 'lives . . . on the blood and flesh of the people'.

His detestation of the destroyers and controllers is so intense that he cannot see the Northmen with the same sympathetic objectivity as the other peoples he portrays. Although he allows the story to move among the invaders, distinguishing characters, and establishing a relationship between the youthful leader Haakon and his grizzled, ruthless adviser Sweyn, the Northmen are seen as an entirely destructive force without moral value. There is none of the rejoicing in their stoic resolution and sardonic courage in the face of death that we find in Eric Linklater's novel of the same period, *Men of Ness*. The Northmen are described as 'strangers and hostile not merely to the folk of that glen but to the earth and to the air, so that their very echo was an outrage' (*SC* 186). No denunciation could be more complete.

The account of the battle on the shore not only has a ferocious power and vividness but spells out clearly the reasons for the Northmen's victory. They are better armed, better organized, more skilful and less impetuous. Piracy is their job. They do it with hard efficiency.

Throughout the book there are sudden flashes of verbal magic which catch the reader's mind. The language at these moments is simple and deployed without extravagance: the playing of a pipe producing 'a sad melody that was like the wine of time in a dark place'; 'small coloured birds cried pink! pink! and flitted'. We are carried through *Sun Circle* by the current of the tale, yet remain continually aware of the powerful presence of the author, not only for the electric emotional charge in the writing, but in the atmosphere of dark tension, illuminated by flashes of lightning – 'the truth', he writes, 'is a flash of intuition that is a flash of lightning ' (*SC* 352).

There is an unpredictable swirl of uncanny and dangerous insight running through the book. For Gunn goes farther than exploring the history of his people and the nature of religion, farther than seeking psychological liberation for himself; he confronts explicitly that terrible ambiguity at the heart of life, the malignancy that is part of 'all Beyond'.

His way out is not, as might appear, Aniel's journey south to find Drust's son to bring him back as leader, it is to create value out of defeat. 'You will even love your own defeat,' says the Master, 'you will turn it into music' (*SC* 358).

The music comes in fact from one of the dwarfish Finlags called Poison, who has stolen the simple playing pipe from a dying Raven. 'But Poison was not beaten. On the contrary, he was inspired' (*SC* 362). As he plays his tune, 'the more terrible he made it the more certainly was he creating the awful brightness of love' (*SC* 364).

There are fundamental lessons to be drawn from *Sun Circle* by Aniel the artist and by Neil Gunn the artist: 'The more he had daringly drawn (evil) spirits of that sort, the less he had feared them', but to be netted by those spirits, and to use them to net others is to destroy the creative light, for 'Without truth the image is trivial and of no account among men'. 'You did not understand truth: you saw it, and its clarity gave you an assurance that was profoundly happy, cool and transparent as a well' (*SC* 365).

Having dealt with the violence of conquest and destruction, and striven for 'the clearness of acceptance', Gunn can turn away from Aniel's confusions to face the worst self-betrayal of Highland history, the Sutherland Clearances, when the people were driven from their homes to make way for sheep.

His way into this disaster, which he dreaded having to confront, was by concentration not on the wielding of male swords and the deploying of intellectual argument, but on the insistence of women to keep life going despite the fury of accident, aggression, greed, and fate. In *Butcher's Broom*, which follows immediately, Dark Mairi is the book's central figure and the source of its strength.

BUTCHER'S BROOM

In tackling the pain and bitterness of the Sutherland Clearances, when during the Napoleonic wars Highland people were turned off their land to make way for sheep, Gunn made the deliberate decision to detach himself from events and write as an observer. This tone proved impossible to maintain beyond the first hundred pages; a blistering irony then became the mask to hide cold rage.

He sets out to state, both explicitly and by exploring specific characters, the values of his people before the Fall into loss of trust and sense of honour.

The first section of the book is unique in Gunn's writing; it subordinates story to scene-setting, description, and evocation of an entire community in a particular place at a definite time. This explanatory mode would turn readers off were the writing anything less than vivid and exact. In fact every page has a vigorous clarity and poetic force which engages the mind with the experience of seeing.

The place is shown through its inhabitants' knowledge of it: 'A sudden vision of this land ... came upon her, the people close to the earth, the children about them, a slow kind of abidingness in it, bare and austere, in the singing March weather.' (*BB* 351).

We are given a view of a traditional society before it is invaded by the passion for change and the lust for profit:

> The women were the more persistent and fruitful workers, and found the males frequently in their way. Many of the tasks about the house they would not let a man perform – even if he had wanted to, which, of course, he did not ... The system worked very well, for the man in his sphere and the woman in hers were each equally governing and indispensable. (*BB* 65)

Indeed, such a system was still alive and well in the crofts of the 1950s.

Butcher's Broom (1934) is primarily a novel about women, and their determination to keep life going however grim the circumstances, even when they have been betrayed or deserted by the men.

Are we being shown a Golden Age which never existed? Gunn does not invite us to see life as an idyll. Existence is hard, balanced on the edge of poverty. There are conflicts, wild outbursts, misunderstandings. The Ministers and their sober God-fearing Elders, bleak with Calvinist piety, are nominally respected by all, but secretly derided by some. Men and girls leave to find work elsewhere; the croft will not sustain them. But Gunn was always convinced that the clan fighting, raiding and feuding which is taken as the history of the Highlands was largely an occupation for Chiefs and their band of young reivers, while the glens that were once occupied and now lie desolate were the home of communities which followed their pattern for survival and ignored the quarrels when they could. His picture of the culture at its best – deliberately presented in contrast to the greed and arrogance of the powerful – can be given in a single quotation.

The central character Dark Mairi, custodian of practical lore and herbal healing:

> had her own five cattle in the herd, her grain and potatoes, and, overall, the providence of her neighbours – the only banking system known to that people, a system that never closed its doors and provided a dividend only for those who had nothing invested. (*BB* 24)

To Gunn the terrible betrayals were these: first, the Chief, seen as 'father of the clan' and trustee for the land, had become by law its sole owner, and often an absentee concerned only with increasing his personal wealth; second, a decree was made that anyone giving shelter to an evicted person would be subject to immediate eviction herself.

A feature of the society which Gunn portrays is the tradition of wisdom acquired by age and experience, and treated with respect by the community as a whole. The Clearances helped to break this down; but if a culture does not produce wisdom in age, and a respect for both, there is something fundamentally wrong with it.

Old Angus says after the disaster, 'We haven't done much harm... They might have left us... It's a desolate thought – to think of all our hearth-stones turning cold and the sheep passing over them... it makes nothing of all we have done... and our forefathers have done, back through time, the very memory of us is wiped away.' (*BB* 349). There is a chilling sentence which summarizes this: 'the grey sheep like woodlice about the desolate hearth-stones'.

This is not a heroic speech. There are no heroes left. The young men are off fighting Napoleon in distant countries beyond knowledge. But Gunn is determined that through his books the 'memory of us' will not be wiped away.

Early in the tale the three main protagonists are pictured together, with a symbolism which has seemed to some critics too overt; to me it is legitimate in its place: 'In the centre of this gloom was the fire and sitting round it, their knees drawn together, their heads stooped, were the old woman, like fate, the young woman, like love, and the small boy with the swallow of life in his hand.' (*BB* 31).

The old woman, Dark Mairi, is unique in Gunn's fiction, but a character closely resembling the girl Elie recurs in *The Silver Bough* and *Bloodhunt*, while the boy Davie is a rebirth of Hugh in *Morning Tide* and as an adult brings us close to Ewan of *The Lost Glen* and Aniel of *Sun Circle*.

Mairi is in a sense a construct, an idea – the dark indomitable, practical maintainer of life, devoid of humour and imagination, rich in lore and survival skills, moving steadily around her familiar world. 'For Mairi did not embroider anything, but dealt with facts, and the more she got at the heart of the fact the more marvellous it seemed.' She is described variously as 'an earthy outcrop in the half dark', 'tight and upright as a standing stone', and 'not going about anywhere so much as having business where she was at the moment'.

Her story is the story of the community and its fate. Each family when evicted has been allotted an uncultivated patch of land, without shelter, on the craggy coast. When she is expelled from her house her treasured meal chest is hurled into the burn, to burst and spill its cargo. She combs the meal from the water with her fingers and lays it on a flat stone to dry, wasting no time in protest or lamentation.

Elie, whose nature is 'tender and generous to the point of softness' is entirely individual and alive, the girl who will always give, and who gives too much, finding herself pregnant and unmarried, with her young man away in the Army because of 'the deep craving in a boy's breast to do what other boys are doing'. She is destroyed internally by pain and the sense of community disapproval, so leaves to seek work, suffering brutal indignities in the south.

Davie becomes first the sensitive boy of *Morning Tide* and then the strangely perverse young man, who cannot bear to be 'touched', defending always the privacy of his secret core. When he and the girl Kirsteen see each other suddenly with the penetrating intimacy which decides their fate, he shies away, 'For solitariness was in his heart and he desired to go into solitary places and be lost.' His closeness to Elie's shame does not seem an adequate explanation for this dogged cruelty.

When at last they do come together, 'They met in the dark secretly. They loved the dark with its hidden wildness, and they triumphed over the light in which men's deeds were deliberate and evil' (*BB* 350) – an odd saying for a writer who later built his philosophy on the spiritual nature of light. Davie's lack of assurance in worldly and social affairs, we are told, is 'masked by a more subtle pride'.

The enemy is given a voice and a chance to state its case: the aristocrat who wishes to 'improve' his land and the developer Heller conduct a conversation in which the arguments for 'progress' are given cogently and succinctly.

The aristocrat makes his case that 'what benefits the country as a whole benefits the people as a whole...what benefits the landlords benefits the nation.... I am going to improve...' and then gives the game away with the declaration 'I simply will brook no interference, in the slightest degree, with my absolute ownership of my own lands.' (*BB* 260–61).

A lawyer/politician tells Heller, when the man is to be tried for exceeding his legal powers in conducting violent evictions, that he will be acquitted because 'our county is finally ruled by a handful of the great English country families.' He is right. After his trial Patrick Sellar, on whom Gunn's character is based, walked from court basking in praise from the judge, despite the damning evidence of witnesses.

Heller himself declares,

> 'The truth is, my lord, that the people of the glens live in sloth, poverty, and filth; the men won't work; the women slave. I saw starved cattle and scabbed ponies and sheep staggering all over the place, picking up half an existence...the sooner (these people) are cleared out the better for themselves and for those who have the right use of their country at heart.' (*BB* 256)

Gunn's explanation for the excessive violence used in clearance is psychologically penetrating: 'Having overstepped the bounds of decency they must go farther and farther, to keep themselves in countenance; while destruction once set loose even in temperate kindly men, feeds on its own wild hilarious lust.' (*BB* 358).

In truth the unpleasantness of feeling which a man has in doing wrong drives him to do worse. Disgust and self-disgust are both destructive.

The book is a mixture of precise, poetic elegy, and a subtle account of looming disaster so powerful that it grows frightening; the malignancy of the world gathers about you as you read. There is, too, a sense of the uncanny, as if something behind your shoulder moves closer by the hour:

> Caught in the centre of these sounds was a small cry that was not a real cry so much as the crying heart of the sounds themselves. Mairi did not like it. It was the voice out of the eddy, the voice left behind. (*BB* 131)

Yet throughout there is a poetry of the real, of life living itself, which combines with the endurance of the women for whom life is a value with unquestionable meaning. 'Light and fire, they say, can never change their nature, which is to pierce the darkness where cruelty is and evil.' We have seen in the story the cruelty of fire, yet feel the force of this simple statement.

Gunn's detestation of the corruption, arrogance and delusions of power come through in passages which contrast starkly with his simultaneous emphasis on individual shame and pride: 'And perhaps here at last in the profound sense of unimportance, of namelessness, lay the quality that drew Elie and Mairi together. Its natural manifestation was an expression of kindness, of giving.' (*BB* 234).

For Gunn this was a difficult subject to face, a difficult book to write, but despite lapses and stretches of explanation too long for an average patience, it is a triumph of literary skill. An actual and spiritual music emerges from the text; the clarity of the words gives strength to this music: 'Lying in her bed, Elie listened to the burn as it came tumbling down through the frosty night from the crest of the silent wood.' (*BB* 189).

THE SILVER DARLINGS

The Silver Darlings (1941), the third and final book in Gunn's sustained struggle with history, is set in Caithness towards the end of the Napoleonic era. Families driven from their inland crofts have been allocated untended plots, without dwellings, on the rocky coast, to starve or prosper according to chance and their own efforts. They venture to sea in search of a livelihood as the herring trade develops and flourishes.

This is a novel in the Tolstoyan tradition, presenting a teeming world in the throes of change and adaptation, with a huge cast of subsidiary characters coming alive and disappearing as the main stream runs on. It has been characterized as an epic of the fishing industry, but it is so much more than this that I find the description misleading. *The Silver Darlings* is a book of journeys – physical, psychological and spiritual journeys – described both intensely from within and objectively from a distance, with a balance and agility which is an achievement in itself: Catrine's walk from Dale to Dunster; Finn's journey to Wick to save his mother from the plague; Roddie's and Finn's voyage from Caithness to Stornoway via the Flannan Isles; Finn's journey to maturity; Catrine's journey from despair to emotional wisdom; the community's journey from destitution to confidence.

Catrine, the most fully developed woman character in Gunn's fiction, fears and hates the ocean which had drowned her uncle. She fights, literally, to keep her young husband Tormad from going to sea.

> He tried gently to free himself from her grasp, but she held on the more firmly. Her strength was astonishing. He made to take a step away. She twisted her legs round his legs, so that he staggered and they nearly fell...he was panting when finally he disentangled himself and left her on the clay floor choking with sobs, her face hidden. (*SD* 11)

This is intense, passionate, embarrassing, and the emotional drive remains ferocious throughout.

While hauling nets at their first serious fishing, Tormad and his crew are hailed by a sailing ship, and watch with innocence as a boat is lowered and approaches. It is filled with an armed press-gang. The young men vanish from all knowledge of the community on shore. 'The sea glittered from Berriedale Head to Loth, vacant in all that space save for one small derelict boat.' (*SD* 30). Catrine's worst fears have been realized.

She leaves the village, with its bitter memories, on the long walk to her aunt's house in Dunster, and her life becomes centred on her son Finn, who is born there. As Finn grows, the story closes in on the dark and dangerous struggles of male pride. The pride is Finn's, Roddie's, and Gunn's. This gives the book a powerful undertow, as if a whirlpool is sucking them down into a dark hole, and Catrine with them.

Roddie, the leading skipper on the coast, wants above all things to marry Catrine, but holds back because Tormad may be alive; Catrine is sure he is dead but has no proof and can make no move. She sees Roddie as strength and security. But Roddie is a Viking. He holds himself in check, but when inner lightning strikes, explodes in the violence of a wild berserker. 'His pleasantness was a mask; the sort of mask one did not try to penetrate. It came and went as required, leaving him with an impenetrably normal expression.' (*SD* 395).

As a child Finn dotes on Roddie, and would follow him anywhere. Catrine tries to make him promise not to follow Roddie to sea, until her Aunt Kirsty, dying, tells her, 'If you put a boy against his nature, you'll warp him. Remember that.' she does. But as Finn develops, Catrine is in constant anxiety, for Finn is jealous of Roddie and Roddie intolerant of Finn.

Finn eventually sails with Roddie and his crew on a stormy voyage. They are lost in the wilderness, ending exhausted at the distant Flannan Isles, lying 'as if the "Seafoam" had brought to haven a boatload of the dead' (*SD* 308). Finn defies Roddie to climb the cliff in search of water and the eggs of sea-birds, to be swallowed as food. 'Roddie, unknown to himself, groaned and sagged...He had plumbed the depths of fear and terror that Finn knew nothing of.' (*SD* 16). What unmans him is dread of being forced to tell Catrine that Finn has fallen to his death.

Gunn himself disliked heights. Is that why there are so many hazardous climbs in his novels? Perhaps it is pride's determination to overcome the weakness, at least in fiction.

Finn's pride is more tortuous. He is in that line of Gunn characters closest in temperament to the author in his youth – Ivor, Ewan, Aniel. When he sees Roddie and Catrine together 'a great awkwardness held his body so that he could not move', and later, 'suddenly he hated what he had seen, hated it in dumb, frightened anger...as if the ghost of his father had come up behind him' (*SD* 176–7). He feels that in some way his mother has betrayed him.

In Stornoway Roddie's tension breaks out in remorseless savagery when his seamanship is questioned, and he half-kills a man in a bar fight. Driven by some intention to restrain him, Finn approaches Roddie, who knocks him down. Finn flings himself at Roddie and the childishness of his attack later preys on his mind – 'that sensitive braggart vanity, that hurt in the pride, that rushing in, that screaming and yelling, that clawing of futility on the figure of terrible magnificence' (*SD* 370). All this he recognizes as the tantrums of youth; a man would hold himself in check. But the recognition only increases his bitterness.

Finn, to complicate matters still further, is in love with the dark Una and with typical reticence and perversity will neither admit it to himself nor approach her in normal friendliness. When he sees her with others, he condemns her for triviality – 'a penetrating hatred of the girl Una assailed him' – and he devises ruses to avoid her. 'She was a sickness he wanted to be rid of.'

This refusal to admit love and affection recurs frequently in Gunn's novels, the fear in a man of 'giving himself away', of losing his identity in another.

When Tormad's death is proven and Catrine and Roddie can marry, Finn begins to hate his mother. 'Sometimes his heart cried out to her but in a moment there would follow a relentless feeling, a deliberate vindictive pleasure in the thought that she was being hurt' (*SD* 492). And again, 'she could weep herself to death for all he cared.' (*SD* 497).

Below these emotional dramas there is a sense of another dimension of events, of intrusions, indications, discoveries, of a fundamental mystery which informs the world, and remains inexplicable. There is a reference in the book to 'that touch of the alien that is at the heart of true wonder'. It will be typical of his work from this point on that wonder is seen as accompanying the true state of being fully awake in the world.

After Tormad is taken by the press-gang, he appears to Catrine in a dream and mounts a black horse which gallops into the waves. This is a traditional vision. She knows then that he is dead.

There are other visions connected in her mind with Tormad. 'It was though in dream, in another life, she heard the words: Blood: rowan-red. The words were soundless, a haunted rhythm, but their colour was bright as rowan-berries or arterial blood.' (*SD* 43). When Finn in his ignorance presents her with a branch of rowan-berries, she faints.

Finn, as a child, falls asleep in the ruined building known as the House of Peace. When he awakes he sees the place as if it were another world. Later, on the same knoll, he dreams of 'the tall figure of an old man in a white cape...The face did not speak to him or move: it just looked...But the look was extraordinarily full of understanding; and somewhere in it there was a faint humour.' (*SD* 214). It is as if the figure knows that the problems of human life are less important than the living imagine. He is not sure afterwards whether he was indeed asleep or whether he was awake.

The Silver Darlings is itself a visionary book, although this aspect of it is rarely mentioned. The real is transformed by a sense of 'something more', which exists as rocks, weeds, flowers, horseflies exist, and must be accepted accordingly.

Finn himself is not named by accident. There are specific references in the text to the Celtic hero Finn MacCoul, which implies that Finn is destined to be a hero for his community. Whether he justifies himself in that role is doubtful, and the oddity of the book is that it is not his seamanship or his adventures which prove his inner vocation, but the very faculty which gave Gunn himself his sense of fulfilment – ability as a story-teller. Finn's solution to the problems set by extreme self-consciousness and male pride was Gunn's own – through story-telling to understand and make use of the very qualities which endangered him.

When Finn's crew lands on North Uist, Finn tells a gathering the story of his climb on the cliffs of the Flannan Isles. Afterwards an old man, a traditional story-teller, approaches him.

'You told the story well. You brought us into the far deeps of the sea and we were lost with you in the Beyond where no land is, only wind and wave and the howling of the darkness. You kept us in suspense on the cliffs, and you had some art in the way you referred to our familiars in the other world before you told of the figure of the man you felt by the little stone house. There you saw no-one and you were anxious to make this clear, smiling at your fancy...It was done, too, with the humour that is the play of drift on the wave...Yet – all that is only a little – you had something more, my hero, something you will not know – until you look at it through your eyes, when they are old as mine....Many a one may come....in the guise of a stranger.' (*SD* 540).

These are the moments which strike a writer unexpectedly out of the creative air. Finn does not know what the old man means. Nor do we. Perhaps he means, among other things, that the tradition knows more than any individual and so is precious. Gunn is aware that even a great novel is 'only a little' unless it is suffused by 'something more' that is not placed there by art, but arrives from its own time and place, not as imagined life but as vision. He himself writes, 'nothing profound is ever finally and materially clear, but only glimpsed in its symbols ...leaving behind the sweetness of delight, as a flower leaves its fragrance'.

From this time forward the emphasis on 'delight' as a realization of that which lies at the heart of life grows stronger. There is always in Gunn a belief in the fundamental goodness of human nature, despite all the evidence he supplies to the contrary; a possibility of awakening from spiritual sleep; and the existence of a path towards wisdom and understanding. Were this not so, what meaning could life have?

It is not mystery or premonition, however, which gives *The Silver Darlings* its peculiar atmospheric force, but writing of a fine exactness which operates like alchemy, transforming ordinary life into a magical freshness. Wonder is embodied in precise observation: 'that busy cold-green drowning sea'; peewits 'drew near and she heard the silken beat of their wings'; the boat 'steadfast in its wooden dream'; porridge granting its benison so that 'their stomachs were divinely poulticed'; Finn 'lost sight of everything but the radiant pearls that fell from the oar blades'. Again and again such felicities strike the mind awake, changing the way we look at things after the book is closed.

The Silver Darlings was so successful that he was badgered to repeat himself, to write a sequel – something he always refused to do. The theme of history had troubled him too long; now the demon had been exorcized. Ronnie, Tormad's friend, survivor from the press-ganged crew, tells Finn, 'Justify your father and look after your mother.' Gunn had justified his father in *The Silver Darlings*. In doing so he had written a powerful traditional novel while retaining his own peculiar sense of time and of what is beyond time. He could go on to the question that now concerned him most: the nature of freedom, the relationship of an individual to an oppressive society, and the contribution which his people's ancient culture could make to the creation of a balance between community and the free human being.

Before this project is examined we must go back from the exploration of history to the books written between *Butcher's Broom* and *The Silver Darlings,* one of which was crucial to Gunn's development.

5

Highland River

Many writers never escape from childhood. Only as a child were they shaken, brought awake, fully engaged with experience, only as a child were they capable of wonder. As a result, only when they return to childhood as a subject are they capable of seeing life living itself with fresh vitality in language and response.

Unless this awareness and sense of wonder can be carried into adulthood, writing must eventually lose authenticity and become prosaic. *Highland River* (1937), which is mainly about childhood, is the book in which Gunn escapes from it. At times the book seems an almost conscious attempt to do so, as if the writer has chosen a method intuitively, and then realized in the course of writing that he is performing a peculiar piece of liberating ventriloquism.

His publishers wanted another *Morning Tide*. That book had broken open the negative melancholy in which he had been locked, and appealed to the public because childhood restored freshness and vigour to his style and perception. Faber suggested specifically that he might try a novel based on the river beside which he had been brought up. The suggestion was inspired by a pleasant, unassuming book centred on a placid English stream which could have given Gunn little to enthuse about. He was never very responsive to suggestion in any case. But the river in the strath always ran in his mind as the source of his inner life, the ground of his education, and the essence of his early experience.

He knew he could not rewrite *Morning Tide*, and hit upon a technique to avoid doing so. He detached himself at two removes from his own childhood in order to engage with it more fully. First, he imagined the book as the character Kenn's memories and reflections upon his younger life. Second, he chose to see Kenn not as the young Neil Gunn, but as the young John Gunn, his immediate junior as brother, and lifelong friend.

Why? Because he knew that in order to encompass his aim he needed to avoid the intense identification which had destroyed *The Lost Glen*. Third, he is even more securely protected by the device of narrating Kenn's story in the third person, while identifying it as Kenn's recollections, so that the narrative voice is ambiguous.

Gunn would not give himself away if he thought he was being watched. To write directly of his own childhood would be to give himself away. But to be entirely open and to recreate experience and the reality of events, he must feel free and uninhibited. He could stand behind John, who in turn stood behind the imaginary Kenn. All three grew up beside the same river.

There was an extra disguise. Although Neil was fascinated by physics and competent at mathematics, he was not a scientist. John had been educated in the sciences, and was a soldier in the First World War. This opened the whole twentieth-century experience to the novelist, for John could supply the most detailed and sensitive account of events and emotions for imaginative recreation.

In fact, of course, the experiences on the river are Neil's own rather than John's. Several recur in Neil's autobiographical *The Atom of Delight*. The feelings, sights, sounds, perceptions, visions are vividly described at first hand.

And indeed, Kenn's story is not the work of a scientist but of a literary artist. The single discussion between Kenn and his chief in the physics laboratory where he works is essentially philosophical rather than scientific. The occasional, deliberate references to past scientists have less resonance than the numerous literary allusions in the text. What exactly is the nature of Kenn's scientific research? We are not told. If this were Kenn's own narrative we would have been, because it would be alive in his mind. No, this is an account of Gunn's own responses to the living world of his childhood, more fully, immediately, and philosophically explored than in *Morning Tide*.

The narrative voice is usually employed with subtlety and skill so that we hardly notice the transitions in space and time.

46

But now and then the manipulation grows awkward: 'But Kenn has an urge to be explicit, even to labour what is infinitely elusive.' Who is speaking here? Undoubtedly it is Gunn himself, to whom this urge is always a strong temptation, and elusive he often proves to be in *Highland River*.

The problem with the book as a whole is that while writing Gunn needed to remember that his readers were less concerned with 'inner meanings' than with action and emotion, but if he himself were not able to follow the quest for these inner meanings the urge to write would leave him. It is in fact remarkable that a book which lacks a strong story-line, involves a good deal of discursive exploration of Highland tradition and culture, and which allows the narrative voice to rove in a variety of directions, should have become both a critical and a commercial success.

That it was indeed successful is a tribute to Gunn's now established readership, which proved willing to follow him in pursuit of many an evasive scent and vision seen by the way. This willingness must have been due to the sensitive vitality of the writing itself, which, as Gunn puts it, 'captures a quality of awareness and delight'. Three examples of the intense yet simple poetry of the book will demonstrate what I mean: of a bird held in the hand, 'The beating of its heart would grow so quick that it was like the pulse of pain in a nerve'; of birds in the trees, 'the odd notes of birds, the little twists of song, like twists of crystal water in sunlight'; of a horsefly: 'The cleg was silent, the colour of old horse-manure, a sort of living ghost of evil.'

The pattern of the book is at once simple and complex – simple because it follows the course stated by Gunn himself, or Kenn himself, or both together:

> Going back from the mouth to the source may seem to be reversing the natural order, to be going from the death of the sea, where individuality is lost, back to the source of the stream, where individuality is born. Yet that is the way Kenn learned his river and when he came to think of it that is the way he learned life. (*HR* 66)

The book is 'an exploration into the source of the river and the source of himself.' But it is complex because of the shifts in time and the shifts in tempo from action to contemplation and back again, a very difficult piece of conjuring to bring off without causing irritation and bewilderment in the reader.

The book begins with the epic encounter of the small boy and the salmon, when Kenn is drawing water from the stream, and is tempted into a battle which results in food for the table and a pair of new boots. Characteristic of Gunn, his love of secrecy, and of the poaching forays which extend Kenn's explorations ever farther up the river, is this paragraph when Kenn first catches his glimpse of the fish.

> So intensely did he listen to the silence that he might well have caught a footfall a mile away...His eyes shot hither and thither along horizons, down braes, across fields and wooded river-flats. No life moved; no face was watching...Out of that noiseless world in the grey of the morning, all his ancestors came at him. (*HR* 11)

All his ancestors come at Kenn throughout the book, to teach him about his nature and the nature of the folk he springs from as he travels towards the source.

He reaches the source at last only when he returns to the strath as a mature man, with both mother and father dead, and the community no longer his own. Many discoveries are made along the way, many insights recorded: 'what ultimately proved to be the memorable things were hardly observed at the time'; '...God, whose power and mystery and terror has been – his silence'; and magic as 'the moment of absorption' which is 'remembered with delight'.

When Kenn stands by the insignificant source of his river he reflects that 'A man had to find himself, had to hold himself with a solitary, lonely integrity'. We are back with loneliness and secrecy as if they were positives: 'a loneliness of secrecy and magic'; 'the river was an adventure often intense and always secretive'. The realization of 'a solitary, lonely integrity', however threatened it may prove to be, is Gunn's escape from the necessity for the recreation of childhood, into a maturity determined to explore the mysteries of the world at large, knowing always the value of 'that momentary ecstasy when thought is lost in pure light'.

6

Casting About

The 1930s was a difficult decade; the pressures of economic depression and the growing threat of war bore heavily on everyone, particularly on artists sensitive to the temper of the time. Accusations of 'escapism' were thrown at those who expressed a naive belief in the goodness of life and the joy of living. It may be that some of these accusations, aimed at *Highland River*, drove Gunn to attempt a confrontation with contemporary social ills and the degradations of urban existence.

This makes *Wild Geese Overhead* (1939), although inadequate as a novel, highly significant in Gunn's literary pilgrimage. The success of *Highland River* gave him the confidence to admit publicly that he was an intellectual, fully capable of expanding and justifying his experiences, and willing to tackle head-on the theme of the day: that the necessity to improve the general condition of society meant the inevitable subordination of the individual.

The experiences he is concerned with in *Wild Geese Overhead* are the epiphany (in its Greek, not its Christian sense) of joy and enlightenment, frequently described in *Highland River*, and the attack on the human mind by the disintegrating force of evil which is recorded in his *Off in a Boat*. It is significant that this book was written immediately before *Wild Geese Overhead*.

The rewards brought by *Highland River* encouraged Gunn to throw up his job in the Civil Service and sail away on a career as full-time writer. But before starting work he bought a motor boat and made his sea-journey down the west coast and round the Isles. *Off in a Boat* is his account of the trip.

49

It includes this passage:

I had been sleeping in the south wing of an old country mansion house when, sometime during the night, I awoke, sat up in bed in a room dim with starlight, and saw my door swing noiselessly open. The transition from sleep to sitting up watching the door open must have been almost instantaneous. I immediately went and stared into the long black corridor, but neither saw nor heard anything. Then I closed the door and went back to bed, but could not sleep, for I became aware – or rather I had an apprehension – of what I may tentatively call pure evil. Now strangely enough it did not come from inside the house but from outside, and not from the ground but from the air, from the vaults of space. It was not a being, a spirit, an imminent presence: it was a force; not a black magic but (if I may be understood) a black electricity. It was quite impersonal, yet not a mere death ray; an emanation from an actual principle of evil, as though the old conception of two principles in creation, good and evil, were in fact true, and the evil was at that moment having an undisturbed innings. The method of its operation was disintegration for its own sake, a disintegrating of the mind, the personality, and finally of the body. Its purpose was to break up the tissue of what the good or creative principle had put together, and one had to strive against it with the utmost strength of one's will. (*OB* 142–3)

The passages in *Wild Geese Overhead* are these:

It was the horror of the outer loneliness, a fear so intense that it curdled away the flesh from the cold bone. He felt himself disintegrating, and fought to keep the strands of his body together...He saw for the first time that he might be beaten, that the forces of the outer darkness might in very fact destroy him. (*WGO* 115–16)

And again:

There, for the first time his life, he realised the existence of pure evil. Not a negative force, like the absence of good, the absence of ethics, of morals, the destruction of custom; but a positive force functioning in its own law and right. (*WGO* 246)

This is an odd and confusing way of putting it, but the sense of evil as a force directed against the personality remains. And the creative principle being equated with 'good' is fundamental to Gunn's view of the world.

Will is a journalist in Glasgow. He walks into the countryside as a release from urban confinement, and becomes a lodger in a farmhouse where his motherly landlady has a niece from the city who appears every weekend to tend the garden. This girl Jenny repels his polite and tentative approaches as if she sees him as an alien intruder, and as a result begins to haunt his mind.

Will continually experiences moments of joy and wonder, always as a result of sudden awakening to the living reality of birds, trees, beasts and flowers, each of which becomes more magical the more clearly he sees them as alive in their own right. The experiences are described both exactly as sights and as realizations experienced: 'A complete freedom, in a gladness that was calm, an ecstasy that was as still as light', or 'that lovely exquisite moment of understanding when you know, beyond all telling, that life is good... that life is creation'.

There are moments when these descriptions become so abstract as to invite question: 'that ultimate apprehension of truth which brought illumination and, in the complete suspension of disbelief, the spirit's clear freedom'. What precisely is an 'ultimate apprehension of truth' and what is the exact nature of the truth which is being apprehended? Any apprehension of 'truth' can surely be expanded or modified by another illumination? And does not the 'complete suspension of disbelief' imply a closing down of that necessary scepticism which prevents deception? This is the kind of statement which leads to accusations of vagueness and 'mysticism', to which Gunn always took exception. To him the apprehension of reality was direct and immediate, arriving through observation and realization of the natural living world before him. When he strove to encompass this in words he often lost readers.

In his newspaper office and the pubs frequented by his fellow journalists, where they drink and argue too much, Will is attacked for 'escapism' and 'sentimentality' by those who resent his assertions of life as a value in itself. Hasn't he seen how people actually live?

Will finds himself accompanying his socialist friend Joe into Glasgow's teeming slums. In Will's hypersensitive state the journeys become a nightmare, with civilization distorted into aberration, fear and degradation. 'The men were undersized and thin, and, with hunched shoulders, seemed to move along on stealthy business'. Secrecy is not seen now as something positive

51

but as sinister and threatening. Will 'imagined (the river's) slow, drowning, rat-coloured swirls, its choking smoothness'.

His effort to find psychological balance puts him under continual tension. One night he gets into a fight, is beaten up, and lies in hospital with no interest in recovery. The doctors confess defeat. He is saved by the kindness of his landlady and her niece Jenny.

This is where the weaknesses of the book begin to tell. First, Jenny never becomes a living reality. She remains a romanticized Primavera of the kind which so irritates feminist critics. Second, his total collapse is not sufficiently motivated, and invites the question: if Will's experiences of epiphany are valid, why do they not protect him from this state of nihilistic defeat? Third, descriptions of the nightmare city may be regarded as a symptom of Will's state of mind, but eventually force us to the conclusion that not only Will but Gunn himself cannot accept urban life as positive, regarding it as repellent and unnatural. In later years Gunn became fully reconciled to Edinburgh as a civilized reality, but it is doubtful whether Glasgow ever lost for him its sinister aspect – witness *The Lost Chart*, written some ten years after *Wild Geese Overhead*. Fourth, there is no doubt that the end is 'sentimental' in the sense of emotion being willed rather than fully realized.

All this does not detract from the interest of the book. The psychical states are vividly conveyed, and the arguments subtle and of their time: if the desire to order society in the supposed interests of its members leads to total control by a machine-state, then the individual will be destroyed and human life made meaningless. This statement of the matter leads straight to *The Green Isle of the Great Deep*, published in 1944.

In the meantime we are left with a number of aphoristic perceptions which resonate long after *Wild Geese Overhead* is closed: 'the question and its answer were one flash of light'; 'You cannot prove life: you can only live it. And living it should be a thrill, a joy'; and his final comment on the thirties poets whose critical attitudes Will has been digesting: 'the poets were right; not the poets who thought, but the poets who, having thought, listened'.

It's entertaining that the novel contains a gentle but cogent analysis of T. S. Eliot's *The Use of Poetry and the Use of Criticism* – a comment by one of Faber's authors on one of Faber's distinguished directors. Gunn wasn't willing any more to be classified as a country cousin.

SECOND SIGHT

Second Sight (1940) has something of an interim flavour. The ideas involved are sound enough as a stage in Gunn's literary pilgrimage. He saw the hunting lodge and its deer-stalking culture as another aspect of 'the spiritual Clearances', with its class-conscious divide between incoming estate owners and the native Highlanders who acted as servants, estate managers and gillies. Since sheep farming had failed and another spate of Clearances had replaced sheep with deer, the situation was one more blow from history and another injury to pride.

Gunn considered that the old Highland culture had something to offer which contemporary civilization had lost. By taking the Highland phenomenon of second sight – the vision of a funeral procession forecasting a specific individual's death – from which members of the community had suffered through the centuries, and combining it with shooting-lodge culture and the competition to stalk and shoot a legendary stag known as King Brude, a story could be written giving a picture of time and place, and highlighting the argument between sceptical science and the pragmatic acceptance by a traditional way of life of inconvenient realities for which no provable explanation exists.

But there were serious difficulties to overcome. Gunn was not at ease with the characters who frequent Highland shooting lodges, and had no intention of writing a comic satire. Although he works hard to create lively dialogue and conflicting positions, the idiom of the exchanges does not ring quite true, and the characters emerge rather as stock figures than living individuals. Nan Shepherd,[1] a sympathetic friend and a novelist in her own right, said in a letter after the publication of *Second Sight*, 'Your English folk never really please me – why I didn't like "The Lost Glen".' Gunn's reply shows the awkward defensiveness of someone who knows she's correct but won't admit it.

The stereotyping of characters is partly due to the remarkable fact that he wrote the story years before as a play, and only when

53

in dire need of a subject transformed it into a novel. James Bridie[2] read the play and wrote a typically forthright criticism, pointing out that the denouement, involving a preposterous practical joke which goes wrong, is both unconvincing in itself and unacceptably melodramatic in a piece of writing with a serious theme. Gunn took no notice at all of this expert opinion and transferred the plot-trick and denouement unchanged into the novel.

The play form hampered him throughout. Characters on a stage can get away with a good deal of stereotyping because living people – actors – embody them, and can bring their own mannerisms and personalities to provide nuance and presence. But to reproduce play-scenes as dialogue in a novel rarely succeeds.

The central intellectual argument, although interesting in itself, is given at a length which may try the patience of some readers. What's more, the sceptic Geoffrey is so disliked, not only by the other characters but by the author himself, that the reader begins to see him as the underdog instead of the representative of society's majority view.

In any case, since we witness the vision of the funeral procession, at least to the extent that Harry, the character with whom we are expected to identify, sees Alick the gillie experience it, the case is already made. Either Alick is a liar or he had the vision. Since the vision was so unwelcome, he is obviously not a liar. The only question is: how to explain the event. The exposition of J. W. Dunne's[3] then fashionable theory of time as the fourth dimension will only convince those already disposed towards acceptance, and the description by another character of the development of latent powers through meditation and specialized disciplines does not apply to Alick, and could in any case only be confirmed by similar experience.

The whole activity of stalking and the way it was carried on at this period is explored with honest ambivalence in a journal Gunn kept in 1939, when *Second Sight* was being written:

> A world in itself – and a very attractive one, were it not kept up by privilege and in the end devoted to preserving life in order to kill it...At one time I was quite fond of shooting. In fact the hunting instinct is one of the strongest in my blood.
>
> I know nothing so exciting, so health-giving, so full of the very

glow of life, as stalking game ... But as sport it will never be of any use to me now. I don't care to see others shooting. I dislike the distant report of the guns ...

He goes on to reflect that war is now largely killing at a distance, and concludes, 'We have raised a mechanism between us and the facts of death. When the mechanism becomes so perfect that it operates almost automatically, it will destroy us.'

In fact it is only in his descriptions of stalking and other outdoor activities, when he escapes from the play formula, that the action is fully alive and engaging.

The difference in tone and intensity between the passionate gloom of *The Lost Glen* and the controlled detachment of *Second Sight*, both books dealing with the same social situation, shows the distance, for good or ill, that Gunn has travelled between 1926 and 1939. But full maturity as a novelist had to wait to display itself until *The Silver Darlings* was published in the following year.

7

Innocence and Dystopia: *Young Art and Old Hector* and *The Green Isle of the Great Deep*

To treat *Young Art and Old Hector* (1942) and *The Green Isle of the Great Deep* (1944) together is to trace the course of a providential accident and to explore the ways in which the creative mind generates thought by setting characters a challenge, as in legend or folk tale.

While struggling with the emotional complexities of *The Serpent*, Gunn was asked by the editor of *Chambers' Journal* to provide a series of short stories. The readership of this durable institution liked outdoor adventure and romance without explicit sex. Dark thoughts were unwelcome. In Gunn's childhood old men and young boys were often in each other's company because neither could do a full day's heavy work in the fields. Why not use this relationship to tell traditional stories to show how knowledge and culture are passed from generation to generation through one-to-one understanding? In *Young Art and Old Hector*, Hector, the old man, is teaching Art, the boy; by the end of the *Green Isle* Art is teaching Hector.

After the stories had appeared in book form Naomi Mitchison wrote to Gunn mildly protesting that, since she had not come across this relationship in the Highlands, could there perhaps be something sentimental or escapist in the choice of subject?

The word 'escapist' applied to anything he had written was a red shirt waved before a Highland bull, and although pride later caused him to deny it, Mitchison's challenge put into Gunn's mind the idea of tackling through the two characters in the stories the most dangerous contemporary threat to human freedom.

56

He had long been concerned with the way in which Stalinist Russia had been using subtle and destructive interrogation techniques to induce sincere devotees of the revolution to confess themselves traitors to the Soviet State. (It was a similar concern which drove Orwell to write *1984*.) How would two disparate representatives of Highland values, Young Art and Old Hector, fare if set down in a sophisticated totalitarian society?

The stories in *Young Art and Old Hector* have enough bite to be interesting for their own sake, but their chief charm is in the relationship between a quick, bright, moody boy, subject to inner turmoil and extravagant tantrums, for which he is frequently walloped by exasperated elders, and the old man, who knows how to divert, entertain, and instruct him in the ways of the world and the customs of the community.

This is the first book of Gunn's in which humour is endemic. He so enjoyed writing the stories that delight is shared with readers. The stories are entirely free from the black struggle with negative emotion and the humiliations of history, yet steer clear of sentiment. Hector had his hands full with Art.

The Green Isle of the Great Deep is a combination of poetic legend and a penetrating analysis of the dangers of analysis – an irony which Gunn would have greatly appreciated. It is also a study of the disease of power: men with the highest moral intentions can follow the logic of power into a rational and destructive tyranny. Control can never be tight enough: peace requires paralysis.

Old Hector embodies the Highland values of loyalty to friends, courtesy, respect for the individual, and a sense of kinship with the natural world. By the subtlest employment of appeals to those values, he can be led into accepting their destruction. Reason in the hands of the master Questioner is Hector's undoing. But something intuitive, irrational, and fundamental resists. Art, on the contrary, does not submit to reason. He runs. He runs because he dislikes the feel of the Green Isle, and because he fears the weightless creatures who surround him. And he keeps on running.

The two of them arrive in a country which bears an uncanny resemblance to home, but is not home. They are in the Gaelic Paradise. What have people made of it? They have made of it a prison in which beings 'like clean empty shells on a strange sea shore' act their allotted parts with shallow obedience.

The natural fruit of the richly laden trees is forbidden. The knowledge of good and evil is forbidden. Obedience is peace and dissent impossible. Instead of natural food, the folk are fed on a drugged gruel which saps the core of will in the living mind. When once the gruel has been eaten real fruit becomes poisonous.

Hector and Art are told by an official Coastwatcher, 'Three days and nights to reach the Seat on the Rock. And each night you will stay at an Inn. You will follow this road and not leave it, nor eat what you may see.' (GI 26).

But Art sees the fruit and eats it with enthusiasm. And they do not stay at the Inn. They spend the night with the woman Mary, who has secretly prepared a herb jelly to counteract the poison, and feeds it to her husband Robert (so named after Robert Burns).

And so the story begins.

The Isle is run by experts in 'Atomic Psychology' who tease the mind to pieces with subtle questions, eventually shaking the sense of truth, undermining the integrity of experience, and darkening the light of intuition. The word 'freedom' has become a meaningless sound.

'You will understand', Robert tells Hector, 'with a new freshness the sin of disobedience. You will realise that obedience is the highest of all virtues, for in it is order, and seemliness, and an end to the burden of thought and decision.' (GI 92). The irony is bitter.

When all is ruled by reason, reason itself has no defences against the relentless application of analysis. To Gunn, salvation lies in the hidden springs of human behaviour, in the lightning flash of insight, and in the growth of wisdom – for 'Knowledge is high in the head as nuts on a tree, but the salmon of wisdom swims deep' (GI 241).

Hector's mode of resistance is essentially Highland, and reference is made to his natural genius for evasiveness. But it is in fact his fundamental respect for truth that the Questioner uses to undo him. If he answers the Questioner straightfor-wardly, then he must betray Mary and Robert. Then the full truth will be torn out of him. If he does not answer, he must have something to hide, and the questioning will continue until he flounders, fails and cracks. Of all things, to betray friends would be for Hector the final shame.

> For torture one can bear to the human limit; but when its end is not the suffering of torture but the degradation of the spirit in treachery then is born a vileness that no eternity can wash out. (*GI* 138)

Mary proves to be the only one able to deceive the Questioner by appearing to be 'cleansed', to have become the 'pale shell of her former being' while retaining her inner essence intact. Continually and repeatedly – in *Butcher's Broom, The Serpent, The Other Landscape* – Gunn places his hope and faith in women because 'a woman always fights not for a theory, not for a system, but for life. For dear life!' (*GI* 91). And if ambition drives women to think and act like men, humanity will fall prey to the analytic reasoner.

Hector, driven to the condition of a wounded beast, cries out at last, 'I want to see God.' He has learned from Robert that this right of final appeal not only exists but is the one rule which the authorities are bound to obey. It is said in the Green Isle that 'the curious thing about God is that He does not seem to hear about anything until it becomes a legend' (*GI* 128). Art, with his mysterious flights, sudden escapes, unexpected appearances, and uncanny speed of foot, has become a legend. And God hears of it. The intellectual champions of Atomic Psychology, the theorists who aim to create 'the corporate mind', are each in turn confounded and put to flight by questions so simple and unexpected that no satisfactory answer exists. As William Blake says, 'The Questioner who sits so sly/ Shall never know how to reply.'[1]

But God's version of the answer to the problems of power immediately raises further questions which the text does not ask. Most of the present administrators, God tells Hector, will be removed from their positions, 'and in their place would come those who had the urge to serve in an administrative capacity and who from time to time would have to consult with the Council of the wise men'(*GI* 245). And the Council of wise men would have no power.

Most of the administrators will be replaced? By whom? Not by the people of the Green Isle, but by the Final Authority, who steps down to break the closed system. Authority to control authority? If all authority has been subject to the corruption of power, how is it that the Final Authority is immune?

Here on earth God directly intervened, according to the Christians, once and for all; this defines the religion. Human experience would teach us that he intervenes only through the insights and actions of living men and women. On their realization of the springs of justice and mercy, the future of life on earth depends.

We are told that the Questioner was once to be counted among the wise. If that is so, will not the administrators appointed in his place eventually go the way of the Questioner? Suppose 'those who have the urge to serve in an administrative capacity' find excellent reasons for not consulting the council of wise men, and conceive effective methods of concealing their activities? The council does not have the power to compel them. And what is this 'urge to serve in an administrative capacity'? Might it not be the very urge to power which caused the trouble in the first place? And where in all this do we, the ordinary folk, come in? No, the solution is not wisdom from the top down, but responsibility from the bottom up. Gunn has not taken his examination far enough.

One of the underlying and unstated assumptions of *The Green Isle* is that paradise is essentially rural. The Questioner and the advocates of the 'corporate mind' – over which, of course, they will have absolute control – represent the rootless urban intellect detached from the natural world, and so live not in the heart but only in the head, dealing in abstractions, theories and statistics.

Art and Hector represent by contrast life lived in touch with the rhythms of nature and the wisdom that derives from understanding the basics of human need, which include freedom and love. But God has always proved difficult to pin down, and the mystery of life and of the human psyche remain.

The way to step beyond all this is seen clearly enough by the author of *The Green Isle*. The integrity of the individual and his deepest insights are the necessary basis for a viable community, whether rural or urban. It is the investigation of relationship between the two to which Gunn increasingly turns his attention.

The total effect of *The Green Isle* does not depend on its argument but on the beauty and resonance of its shafts of perception, the brilliant clarity of its language, and the astonishing force of its imagery.

As Hector stands listening to the voices of hounds and men in pursuit of the fleeing Art, 'The night itself heard, and shivered like broken glass in all the far windows of space.' (*GI* 188). And again, 'all the words were like birds in the air, excited birds that could not land. When Robert stood still, however, all the cries died away, and the words came to rest on him as on a dark tree. The upward gleam of his eyes gave space to the tree and invisible branches.' (*GI* 124). Robert, of course, is a poet. So is Gunn. He is a poet who makes explicit in this book the lessons he has learned through living and through writing:

> For love is the creator; and cruelty is that which destroys. In between is the no-man's land where men in their pride arrange clever things on the arid ground. (*GI* 204)

Literature has often been the no-man's land in which men arrange clever things on the arid ground. Gunn had lost interest in all that. He wanted to write of essences, of what matters fundamentally if life is to have meaning.

8

The Mature Novelist

Neil Gunn wrote in a letter to F. R. Hart, 'The Serpent...is one of my own peculiar ones about which I'd say nowt.' Academic critics seem to agree, for the book has received little detailed attention. In fact it is central to Gunn's work and marks a distinct phase in his development. The story gradually attains the force of myth from the depths of a clairvoyant understanding.

It is in some respects the most dramatic and moving of his novels, heavy with dark incident but in the end profoundly positive. Gunn has gained the ability to write from 'elsewhere' while probing empathically the deep reality of emotional crisis.

For the first time he can confront head-on the negative aspects of the Highland community rather than concentrating on the disruptive effect of alien forces. Oppressive Calvinist dogma is used by hell-and-sin-fixated elders as a weapon to boost their power and self-importance. The conflict between the individual need to arrive at a personal vision of the world and this form of intellectual tyranny is embodied in the conflict between Tom, nicknamed 'The Philosopher', and his jealous, brooding father.

There are two other themes which run through the book: one is Tom's relationship with his loving, inarticulate mother, the other his affair with Janet, the girl who follows her own nature to betray him, sacrificing loving friendship for passion.

Tom's inner confidence is destroyed by the blame which the community lays on him for the death of his father, and by his grief and bitterness at Janet's desertion. He is rescued from this psychological breakdown by the total devotion of a mother whose lack of intellectual ability has irritated him for years.

The book is written after the pattern of *Highland River*, with Tom reviewing and recreating in his last days the desperation and fury of a turbulent youth, which he can now see with tolerant detachment. The method is used more directly and effectively than in *Highland River*, so that the transitions from story to reflection are managed with a straightforward honesty which makes changes of tone and mood seem as natural as breathing.

Tom is not in essence 'the Gunn character' with whom the author tends to identify, but a more kindly, generous figure whose nature is threatened by bitter loneliness, guilt, and grief. Tom is alive and solid, and his collapse one of the most penetrating psychological studies in Scottish literature. The final philosophy by which Tom as 'the Philosopher' navigates the world is expressed with a simplicity not always evident in Gunn's writing.

Tom goes from the Highlands to Glasgow to work. There he is involved in the socialist and sceptical furore of the late nineteenth century. Traces of the city nightmare can be seen in the Glasgow episodes, but the Philosopher's summary closely resembles the way in which Gunn preferred to see his own youthful sojourn in the urban wilderness of London: 'He had observed the scene with an extreme clarity, taking part in it as far as need be, but something in him had held him back. Thus he had often enjoyed its fun to the highest degree but with the watcher's enjoyment, with a queer liberating detachment' (S 159).

Tom returns home to run the croft when his father falls ill, and is always conscious of the oppressive dominating power which the father exerts, based on detestation of his son's ideas, ambitions and even his abilities. The father's weapons are silence, illness, and brooding, looming disapproval.

After a dispute with his father, Tom sees his mother emerge from the house and 'made a move to avoid her, but she ran out a step or two, a waddling creature with an anxious face, near on tears, a thick husky voice going thin..."Oh, Tom, bear with him, bear with me." ' (S 69).

The climax comes when Tom is engaged in a dispute with one of his father's righteous friends.

> There was a shuffling of feet in the doorway. Tom turned and saw his father before him.

The grey face, the grey beard, the blazing eyes, the silent pursuing face – it had come at last. The power of the father created in the image of God. The tribal power, the unearthly power. Each felt it, and Tom could not move.

The father gazed upon his son with a fixity of expression more terrible than all words. In silence he groped for William's staff. He took a slow step nearer to his son, and, in the short pause that followed, the intention of chastisement gathered in a concentration horrible to behold. Then the hand with the staff went up, not quickly, but with deliberation. It rose, until it rose high above his head, then all in a moment the stiffness of the arm slackened, the stick fell, bouncing off Tom's chest, the arm wavered down, the body sagged, and with a deep soft grunt it collapsed upon itself, pitching forward slightly before Tom's feet.' (S 170–71)

Tom becomes an outcast from the community, which blames him for his father's death. When he discovers Janet's involvement with the son of the manse, he descends into darkness and hallucination, seeing his dead father looming in the field, Janet's haunted face, and in the night terrible, malign beasts fixing him with a cold, destructive stare.

The reconciliation with his mother is so subtly, objectively done that no question of sentimentality arises, there is only the closest and most scrupulous attention.

The need to look after him had brought all her working energy back into full play... There was nothing too much for her to do...

And she never knew the right thing to say. Never. But she kept on working, with an endurance nothing could break... (S 208)

When the visions become intolerable and he screams aloud, 'Her arms were round him. "No one will get you!" she cried'. Later, 'The qualities in her that had formerly made him impatient with her were the very qualities of endurance and patience which he now saw were the only ultimates against the cruelties and inexhaustible resource of fate.' (S 211).

The final drama occurs when Janet's demented mother strikes her down, furious at discovering that the daughter is pregnant. One passage in this episode stays in the mind long after the book is closed.

It was then she gave him that strange white look that haunted him for years. There was loneliness in it, something wild and scared. It glistened distantly from him yet came into him and burned him up.

It was more than a farewell in its glistening anguish. And from somewhere in the heart of it she smiled to him.' (*S* 248)

There is a poetry in Gunn's writing which is not a matter of words but of perception. Sometimes the words explicitly express and illuminate the perception, sometimes they have an evasive quality which confuses the reader, but the perception itself strikes home as authentic.

Tom the Philosopher's final meditation makes plain that Gunn himself has realized that the chief enemy to integrity of perception is the negative emotion which features so strongly in *The Grey Coast* and *The Lost Glen*. He is using *The Serpent* (1943) to fight it through the beleaguered Tom. As Tom explains to his dying mother, who is still troubled by the community's ministers of gloom, 'We just do our best according to our natures, and there's no more we can do. And if Christ was kind it was because he understood.' (*S* 278)

She murmurs 'I'm so happy', 'life sinking away from her like water through sand'.

To the shepherd, Tom explains, 'For at the end of the day, what's all the bother about? Simply about human relations, about how we are going to live one with another on the old earth.' (*S* 201). And that's a ticklish problem when we consider the nature of power in the world and the depredations of the egoistic will.

Tom confronts his own death with the thought, 'For if there was no death, then all is life. And if, at the end, there is death only, then here is life's greatness and its beauty.' (*S* 279).

But there is something beyond this. The mystery remains, and Tom is ceaselessly aware of 'the extreme pause when it seems that the veil which divides being from not-being becomes filmy, verges on complete translucence'. At the end, too, there is this characteristic Gunn reflection: 'It is the ultimate gaiety that comes from a knowledge of loneliness.' There is strength in this.

The Serpent of the title is variously explained as the earth-spirit, as eternity, and as wisdom, but of course to the elders of the Kirk it represents the wiles of Satan. Tom is identified with that serpent. The Philosopher emerges despite them as a whole man in his own right and the book as a drama of darkness and understanding.

THE KEY OF THE CHEST

The aftermath of the Second World War was clouded by tension between the Western powers and the Soviet Union, where the repressive Stalinist regime was in full control. It's not surprising that Gunn's attention was centred on the significance of freedom, both as an individual drive and as an operative principle in society. *The Key of the Chest* (1945) followed immediately on *The Green Isle*, and concerns itself with the ways in which individual and community interact. If the community is oppressive or too intrusive, or if individual behaviour grows too unbridled, both suffer.

During his lifetime the Highland community had been deeply damaged by economic decline and the loss of its younger and more active members. *The Key of the Chest* examines its chances of survival, not only as a culture in its own right, but as a paradigm of human society as a whole.

The novel is again experimental in that the third-person narrative is conducted from several points of view, and characters are introduced whose function is to observe, interpret and comment on action and events. The transitions from one viewpoint to another and one milieu to another are managed with such confidence and unobtrusive skill that the effect is one not of detachment so much as balance and control.

The story is set in the years before the First World War. Charlie MacIan, yet another of Gunn's returning failures, has lost his faith and sense of purpose, and thrown up his course of training for the ministry. His return is especially shameful because he has been helped to university by local benefactors, particularly by the sacrifices of his brother Dougald, shepherd to the community sheep club. The minister's daughter Flora is also in trouble for meeting him secretly, and after dark, thus defying university rules.

When on a night of storm a ship is wrecked on the coast, Charlie rescues a seaman, who dies. Medical examination shows that he died from strangulation. Was his death accidental? The seaman was clinging to a chest, but since the chest contained nothing of value, why did he save it? Did it once contain money? How is it that Dougald is suddenly able to buy sheep of his own?

On one level the focus is on the mystery – but there are other levels: the basic level of nature, with the moods of sea, wind and weather, and the behaviour of birds and beasts, kept continually under observation; there is the level of the community seen as an operative organism; there is the level of relationships – between Flora and Charlie, between Flora and the minister, between Charlie and Dougald, and of the brothers with the society from which they now feel themselves isolated; then there are intelligent and prying outsiders analysing the community and its behaviour. Finally, there is the metaphysical dimension of meaning.

It is said during the story, 'A living community always meets.' This community meets in three centres: Kenneth Grant's shop, where business is conducted; Smeorach's house for social gatherings; and at the Kirk on the Sabbath.

Kenneth Grant is the organizing brain of the working community, the driving force behind the cooperative sheep club, and all the other progressive moves in the place.

Smeorach's is the only house where the thrawn Dougald calls on visits to the township, and the only house where young and old feel free to mingle. Smeorach is the tribe's facilitator. He is not authoritative and prescriptive like the minister, but an easer of social life, who has a feeling for the traditions of the community, and shows at all times both courtesy and hospitality.

On several occasions, though, we see him suffering from the kind of ennui and despair which the Highland community in general has suffered since the Clearances. Waking in the night:

> Smeorach lifted his eyes to the blind window, and it seemed to him that life was all shadows, and the movement of shadows, and blindness, and had no meaning, and when you hearkened for its sound, it had no sound. (*KC* 78)

The community is an organism with eyes – 'Eyes, many eyes, looking round corners.' No one is safe from observation. Nothing can remain secret. Every event is noted, commented on, remembered.

Someone is watching when Michael Sandeman, the maverick denizen of the Big House, takes his prying photographs of birds and people. His camera is watching them; they are watching him.

The boy Hamish is innocent of knowledge, yet seems to be everywhere, seeing everything. He is watching when Michael goes over the cliff, and it is Hamish who runs for help.

When Charlie MacIan 'secretly' meets Flora, Michael, the doctor, and Michael's friend Gwynn, all see them.

When Dougald MacIan drives home his suspect sheep, Hamish sees him.

When he moves the sheep on the forbidden Sabbath, the minister sees him. When he and the minister clash, eyes are everywhere.

When the minister pursues the lovers, Hamish and his friend Norrie see them.

The doctor sees Flora's final parting from her father.

Typically: 'His mother had heard him coming a long way off. As indeed did the neighbours, who would be wondering what kept the doctor all day.' (KC 39).

The seeing is intrusive, but it saves Michael from death on the cliff, and again when he sets out in a storm to seek Charlie and Flora.

It breaks both ways: curious eyes are always watching, to help or to hinder. Everyone – or nearly everyone – knows everything – or nearly everything. What they don't know, they want to find out. Community is at once a protection and a prison.

When an event occurs, people gather as if by instinct: 'A man here and there found he wanted an ounce of tobacco at Kenneth's, and some of the women thought they might as well buy their messages early, for it was a fine morning.'

The men of the community gather to attend the seaman's funeral, from a sense of respect and hospitality to the stranger.

There are those in the community, however, who are not full members of it, but set apart by position and function – the minister, the doctor, and the policeman.

The policeman must do his duty with regard to the seaman's death, but meets resistance when he enquires where Dougald got the money to buy his sheep. He is worried by the affair not only for his own sake, but for the community's.

And there is the strange position of the minister. The community meets in the Kirk on Sunday but never feels entirely at home there.

The minister is shown at his most caring and his most forbidding within a few pages. He is found giving spiritual comfort to a dying woman; but as he leaves the house he encounters Dougald driving those questionable sheep – on the Sabbath. In the minister's eyes that is a crime.

'Rage at what he saw, black hatred of its abominable desecration, had him in an instant. That a man, accursed already, should so dare!' (*KC* 144).

Later, in the pulpit he denounces the offender, and 'Mr Gwynn had the impression that he began visibly to swell as he took upon himself the powers of judgement and condemnation, under the avenging hand of God' (*KC* 151).

Gwynn is a highly philosophical visitor, who says of the minister: 'He is pulling the boat widdershins...He is doing it deliberately. He is going to smash the superstition...But the superstition stands for a whole way of life. He is therefore smashing that. And what is he offering in its place? Not a new way of life, here and now, but...the salvation of the soul in a future life.' (*KC* 127–8).

The minister then, is at once an anchor for the community, and a threat to it. He should be the link between the people and the spiritual reality of God, but his God is a judging, divisive God, so that religion, instead of uniting the folk, divides them into elect and damned, into theological categories unknown to the traditional way of life.

The minister's relationship with his own daughter is shown as unhealthy. There is a dangerous element of the sexual in his extreme possessiveness.

When he loses his daughter he collapses and is lost, finding his way to Smeorach, the elder of the old tribe, not the new, the tribe whose values were established before the coming of the God of wrath and judgement.

The doctor is at once a link with the outer world of education and science, and a working member of the community. As a result he is the book's central figure.

'The doctor was well liked and considered very able. Women talked of him confidently among themselves.'

But he is set apart by his advisory and authoritative function. Also, his relationship with the outsiders Michael Sandeman and Gwynn indicates a certain separation from the community.

There is continual reference to the doctor's habit of distancing himself from people and events – for example, from the Procurator Fiscal, whose official function it is to investigate the seaman's death: 'though (the doctor) recognised the necessity for officials and their procedures, he usually adopted in their presence a cool and precise form of talk or answer'. This would be very much Gunn's own attitude in such circumstances.

The doctor distances himself, too, from the incomers, despite his willingness to socialize with them. When he sees Michael's photograph of the dead seaman, 'Deep in him there was a movement of that sense of shock, which causes at a still deeper level, a cold stirring of the elements of hostility.' (*KC* 64).

He reacts against the sophisticated abstractions of the philosopher Gwynn. He is afraid, like so many Gunn characters, of 'giving himself away', of letting Gwynn or Michael inside his mind. This characteristic incites satirical comment from the iconoclastic Michael.

Although demonstrating – as Gunn himself does – skill at rational analysis, the doctor distrusts it, reflecting at one point that it can become an effort to 'explain away' what is important but inconvenient. He senses that if analysis goes too far, separation of individual from community is complete, and both are in danger.

Michael Sandeman, the first of the outsiders, is accurately placed in relation to the community. He occupies the lodge which belongs to the landowning family, but is not the family's representative so much as its black sheep, sent into Highland exile. His insight is genuine, but reckless, and his remarkable photographs can seem so intrusive as to be inimical.

When Michael is forced to recognize the existence of community as the result of being rescued from danger by the men of the district, he reacts with a kind of half-humorous generosity, giving the boy Hamish his fishing rod, but making on the second occasion a grievous mistake by offering his rescuers money. He is forced by their courteous refusal to acknowledge a code which has power over the whole social body, and he resents the fact.

Gwynn, the other outsider, has a concern and a thesis. He is looking at the community for elements of the primitive, because, he says, in primitive society, 'life was completely integrated'.

In the modern world, on the contrary, 'The spontaneous belief that gave wholeness is gone. Now if one could grow a new whole out of scientific inquiry and material phenomena alone, then we could see our way ahead. But apparently we can't.' (*KC* 206).

Indeed we can't, and that is one of the main themes of Gunn's writing from this time on.

Gwynn points the danger: 'The need to feel good must in nature have an outlet. When it doesn't get it... then it bursts through with mad scaldings and bloody wars.' (*KC* 207).

Here is the problem. You cannot convincingly advocate freedom without a belief in what Gwynn calls 'the old primordial goodness of the human heart'. To liberate human beings you must trust them. Authoritarians prefer original sin.

Throughout the book myth is brought in to deepen the nature of events, and as a balance to the abstractions of Mr Gwynn. In the minister's case we hear 'Dark and archaic words out of the mouths of prophets, with the power in them of the sign and the symbol... the avenging power that hunts the fleeing heels of sin into death's uttermost abyss' (*KC* 151).

Dougald is said to be 'challenging the forces of the night', and is proven to be indeed 'his brother's keeper'.

Of Charlie playing the pipes at night we hear that the great tunes and laments were so far beyond human power to produce, that the tradition talks of their being granted by 'the small wise people of the green hills' (*KC* 134).

Again and again there are characterizations which depend upon poetic force rather than intellectual clarity – 'Death, dark and round-shouldered with hidden face'.

The Highland community was failing throughout Gunn's lifetime because it had not come to terms with the economic organization necessary for life in the twentieth century. More than this, he had the sense that community all over the Western world was failing, and the strength of the State is no substitute, for community cannot be imposed from above.

What is the meaning of social life in a dying community? The book charts how individual behaviour relates to communal values, and how the two balance. Charlie tells the doctor at the end, 'even if I had children, and grandchildren, they would still be known as coming from me, and beside me always... would be the strangled seaman, and the money' (*KC* 255).

71

It is the mythic, the symbolic, which cannot be overcome. Charlie will leave, and the community be the poorer for it. Human tragedy lies with the inevitable, with the things that cannot be put right. Life goes on, and must go on; the doctor looks for comfort to the permanence of the natural world.

But is that enough? Is it enough for him to live with his mother and tend the sick? Is the community more likely to flourish at the end rather than the beginning of the story? It is to the outsiders, Michael and Gwynn, that the doctor turns for conversation, not to the people of the community, and Michael and Gwynn are birds of passage.

Michael does offer to help Kenneth with future projects, and says at one point that he has had 'a premonition of wholeness'. But Michael is erratic, and this personal wholeness, if ever achieved, will be achieved elsewhere.

For a community, wholeness might be defined as an accepted way of life which provides a sense of meaning and fulfilment for its members; it may begin to break up when too closely questioned and analysed.

The Key of the Chest cannot be said to have anything as straightforward as a message. But it does have a philosophical attitude to the world. The integration of the individual helps the community to thrive, and one function of a thriving community is to help the individual towards wholeness.

The book invites reflection, and leaves us with a sense that the search for meaning and integration will go on because it is essential for the human psyche that it does, and that, whatever happens to a particular people in a particular place, community will restore itself because the species requires it.

THE DRINKING WELL

The Drinking Well (1946) can be seen as a traditional novel which sets out to do for hill sheep farming what *The Silver Darlings* did for fishing in the Moray Firth – a step backward, then, from the experimental and philosophical approach of *The Green Isle* and *The Key of the Chest*, and one warmly welcomed by publisher and public.

But it can be seen in another light altogether – as an extension of *The Key of the Chest*, which it immediately follows, in its examination of the positive and negative aspects of community. Iain Cattanach, another example of the returned scapegrace – this time resurrected from a bleak and gloomy short story written in the 1920s – has been driven reluctantly to desert his father's sheep farm and take work in an Edinburgh law office by his mother's obsession with the need to 'get on in the world', and her detestation of the limitations of Highland life.

The city scenes make some use of Gunn's own early experience of office work in Edinburgh from 1909 to 1911, although Iain's sojourn takes place during the 1930s. The capital and its movements and customs affect Iain at first as an illusory nightmare in which he wanders without aim or purpose: 'What happened in the city bore about as much relation to that reality as one of his copied letters to the actual property it described,' (*DW* 170), Iain's reality being the wind and weather of the hills where the sheep follow their noses in search of food. He protects his 'solitariness, as of a hill-bird', as though 'to lose its tightness would be to lose his strength'. He feels he must 'keep himself within himself and give away as little as possible'.

It is at the point when he is emerging from this defensive isolation that disaster strikes. Before he left home he was suspected – wrongly – of pushing the factor into the river when poaching. From the office he takes off for home after knocking a malignly anti-Highland colleague through a glass door. Obviously, then, a dangerous rough, and a disgrace to the rural community.

'The gossiping word went from mouth to mouth; the eyes watched. He saw the spirit, the positive living spirit, being eaten by it, just as the maggots of the blowfly or green-bottle ate the sheep.' (*DW* 400). Iain complains that 'There's something wrong, wrong and small, with our old country', and 'It's the weakness of the Highlander. Not a damn thing can he do until he's roused.' But Iain is not the Ewan of *The Lost Glen* and Gunn is not now the bitter man who wrote it. Iain can be treated with greater critical detachment – 'suddenly he realized – it was his own conscience that was making him angry' – and is not only roused, but struggles to arouse others, and to find a way out of community decline, preaching practical methods of restoring health to the land, and of reviving sheep farms in a deprived countryside.

The story is rich in incident – over-rich, perhaps, as burden after burden is laid upon the hapless Iain – and there are memorable scenes imagined with emotional depth and in visionary detail: Iain borrowing the fiddle from an old busker and playing the music of the Highlands in an Edinburgh street with such verve that passers-by are inspired to dance; and Iain driving over the hills a flock of hungry sheep through a prolonged and savage snowstorm.

As always with Gunn, the book is much more than an exercise in romantic realism. Not only is psychological penetration uncomfortably deep, but a myth haunts the story. Mad Mairag lives alone, a butt for mischievous children, speaking in riddles and delivering sly prophecies. She is also the guardian of a well which we come to see as the well of wisdom, the well at the world's end. Iain dismisses Mairag as crazy, yet he dreams of the well, and it is there that he returns with the dark Mary at the end of the book. It is characteristic of Gunn that Mary has always known that what Mairag sees is true.

There are passages in *The Drinking Well* where the author seems to be forcing a poetic tone, with such inversions as 'Dark it looked', and 'High the sky was', but every few pages authentic, unselfconscious phrases produce in the reader a sense of wonder and delight: 'The song over, a tiny brown body flicked swiftly here, there; a fern frond moved, and the wren was gone. The whole fern-face looked at him from the shadow,' or 'The cock, vastly astonished, skated on a grey film of ice.' These are the observations of a writer who sees with vivid exactness and knows intimately what he is talking about.

Gunn himself commented on *The Drinking Well*, in a letter to Naomi Mitchison, as if he saw the book as a preliminary to the spiritual exploration which he now knew to be his primary purpose: 'There is such a lot of clearing work to be done so that writers coming after us may take a lot for granted and get on with what may be spiritually exciting.' (*SL* 87).

In the book itself it is said 'We should be done with satire. The best of us have lived on satire too long.' (*DW* 242) Satire is negative, irony dispiriting. It was goodbye to all that. Gunn's confidence was now so strong that he could ask in *The Drinking*

Well the naive and fundamental question, 'Is life worth living?' and to reply in effect, Yes; it's not only worth living, but to be celebrated through every trial, in music, personal love, and the work to which each of us feels dedicated, as well as through close attention to the world itself. He understood the meaning of folk tales, which tell us that the well is real and the water nourishing.

9

Explorations

THE SHADOW

The Shadow (1948) follows the path made by *The Green Isle* in its attack on the effects of analytic reason used as a weapon of destruction. It was written at a time when to be a communist was fashionable; Gunn knew several devoted disciples of Marx.

Nan, who spent the war years in London, is staying in the Highlands with her Aunt Phemie to recover from a nervous breakdown. The first section of the book consists of her letters, most of them never sent, to her lover Ranald in the city. The second section deals with Ranald's visit to the patient, and his spiky relationship with Aunt Phemie.

Ranald is a ruthlessly intellectual Marxist who despises emotional weakness and defines freedom as the recognition of necessity. As Phemie reflects, 'A person like Ranald could talk to the men there, to the farm workers, and find out about everything, and have a scheme for putting things right, but he does not somehow care for the men themselves.' (*SH* 218). His merciless precision excludes the very qualities which make human life emotionally meaningful.

Nan has acquired from Ranald's revolutionary coterie a horror of this world of Know-Alls. She explores the fields, hills and streams, observing every detail of light and life in an effort to dispel the shadow from her mind. The observations are fresh, sharp and delicate – they are in fact those which Gunn himself had been making throughout the war years for a column in the *Scots Magazine* designed to reassure folk under the stress of bombing, privation and worry, that the natural world is permanent and alive. These notes were eventually published in book form as *Highland Pack* in 1949.

Two events shake Nan's growing confidence: the savage murder of an old man in the neighbourhood, and a series of meetings with a predatory artist whose passion for immediate gratification is as deadly in a contrasting way as Ranald's cold intellectual arrogance. A final meeting causes Nan's collapse, and the letters cease.

There are passages in the letters which hold attention and refresh the mind – 'The yellow crocus was a tuning fork out of some sunny underworld, still holding the glow of the note' – and her veering moods of joy, terror, wonder and dismay are described with a hallucinatory force. But although the emotions themselves strike home as valid, the tone can cause sudden doubt and withdrawal. For example, a young woman might cry out in conversation to her lover the words 'Oh, Ran, Ran!' but would she write them down on paper not once but several times?

There are other problems. Both Ranald the intellectual idealist and Adam the artist seem programmatic rather than real. If you met Ranald, his cold rationality would contribute to the effect of his presence, but on paper it dominates to the extent that he fails to lift into life. Adam too is invented rather than known. His responses seem extravagant to the point of being arbitrary. For example, he tells Nan of his vision of the woman Helen going out in the evening to 'fold up the day' and to see that 'the lamp of the moon is trimmed'. This is a beautiful and humorous imagination of Gunn's when staying with Helen and Keith Henderson, and authentic in that context, but totally out of character for the ferocious and devouring Adam.

Aunt Phemie, on the other hand, is vigorously alive. Based on his wife Daisy, she is full of warmth, and rich in firm common sense.

The story holds attention, the dramatic incidents are credible, and the ongoing argument between Ranald and Phemie still of value today. As Phemie remarks:

> 'You may flatter yourself that you have a monopoly of logic. That may be your particular illusion. And more horrors are committed, I'm beginning to think, in the name of logic than in any other name.'
> 'Even God's – remembering history?'
> 'Even God's,'' said Aunt Phemie. (*SH* 119)

Phemie reflects: 'Men had gone mad ... Her vision went all over the earth and saw men in the logical movements of their madness, stalking here and there, into council chambers and out of them, across fields, all the fields of the world, intent and certain, fulfilling the high and urgent law of necessity. Whose necessity? cried her anguished spirit' (*SH* 207).

Despite its power and purpose, the book remains an experiment rather than a triumph. What it shows with great clarity, however, is how definite Gunn's position had now become, how sharp his awareness of the opposing dangers of negative emotion and of ruthless analytic reason, both leading to cruelty, which is the final treason against man.

THE SILVER BOUGH

The Silver Bough (1948) was published immediately after *The Shadow* and, significantly, in the year George Orwell intended for *1984*. The story itself, although in tone and method essentially a comedy, asks and answers a question which troubled many people after the revelations which followed the Second World War: 'What can justify human life, or make it worth living, to one who has seen the depths of cruelty to which men can descend?' This question is centred in the character Martin, but the book carries easily a whole treasury of varied meanings, and is filled with Highland light.

The central figure, Simon Grant, is an archaeologist who makes the remarkable discovery of a gold hoard in an ancient burial cairn – and immediately has it stolen from him.

Grant is a sympathetic, impulsive, irascible, humorous and kindly enthusiast, whose story tempts the appetite with hints, clues and intimations until we are following his darting zigzag progress with a consuming desire to know what happens next. The story itself bears in its bloodstream the message that not only are all the disparate strands essential to its nature, but the story is actually going somewhere, and the somewhere to which it is going will prove of such importance to us personally that we must stay awake and alert so as not to miss anything.

The Silver Bough takes a grip and casts its spell from the first sentence: 'Simon Grant, who had handled many skulls in his time, was immediately taken by the shape of the head, the colouring, and the fineness of the features.' (*SB* 9). We are asking questions already: Who is Simon Grant? Who is he looking at? Why is he accustomed to handling skulls? What's so significant about the shape of this skull? If the writer had given answers – saying, perhaps, 'Simon Grant, the archaeologist, looked with interest at his neighbour in the bus' – we would not have been tempted to read on.

When Grant speaks to his neighbour there is something disconcerting in the man's expression. He seems 'hard, solitary', and 'like a standing stone in an arid waste'. The mention of a standing stone is another hook. We begin to guess at Grant's profession.

When Grant asks the man if he knows 'Mr Donald Martin, of Clachar House', to whom he has a letter of introduction, the man says yes, but Martin is not at home. Later, in answer to an enquiry, the manageress of the hotel points out to Grant the figure of Donald Martin on the road. 'It was the man who had sat beside him on the bus.'

We are led on through a series of such small shocks and surprises with an increasing sense that soon a larger shock, a revelation of light or darkness will suddenly be made, and we will share Grant's elation or discomfiture – and his treasure. If Martin were not to be central to the tale this introductory passage would be illegitimate. But we have confidence in the writer from the start. Every figure and place and function recurs and grows significant at its proper time. The pattern lives and moves.

The ingredients of legend – the Silver Bough, 'a passport to the other world', which, when it is shaken 'sweet music sounds and all sadness, care and sorrow departs from all who hear it'; the Crock of Gold, a treasure which is only to be found at the end of the rainbow – seem entirely natural in their setting, and are not only rooted solidly in human psychology, but relate to what is discovered in the burial mound, which can be measured, photographed – and stolen. Each of the series of interlocking tales has its own logic: Grant and his unique find; Martin, his terrible past, his present withdrawal, his relationship with a neurotic sister; the girl Anna and her illegitimate child, seen sleeping in the sun arranged exactly as are the two skeletons

Grant finds in an ancient cist (an imagined picture which fascinated Edwin Muir);[1] the child and the story of the silver bough; Foolish Andie, Grant's indefatigable and not-so-simple labourer, with his passion for glittering trinkets...There are continual correspondences in time and situation; the present and the past reflect one another; myths born long ago in the human mind prove their power to reveal and reconcile within the patterns of today. Gunn's view of history becomes clear – a human story enacted in time yet embodied in myths which have a timeless meaning. Aphorisms arise in the story like features in the landscape – 'Equations were the chambered cairns wherein the ancient magics were buried', and 'God was "given", like a mathematical axiom, to man in the beginning'. And why, we are asked at one point, should man be said to have 'fallen'? Has he not in fact climbed, isn't it his destiny to learn and make mistakes and discoveries?

Gunn wrote to his enthusiastic but puzzled publisher, Geoffrey Faber, about *The Silver Bough*,

> I don't want an incident or character to be ambiguous or difficult, not even mysterious!...But actually the book is full of symbols or bits of myths. Accordingly there is nothing that the reader cannot go on thinking or wondering about. (*SL* 96–7)

Just so. These 'symbols' and 'bits of myths' provide the links which not only unify the different strands of story, but refer back to deeper meanings which live just on the edge of consciousness.

Grant goes through a series of adventures – accidents, storms, pursuits, arguments, discoveries, and a siege by journalists and sightseers – but throughout is aware of movement beyond his immediate vision, beyond anything that an archaeologist can soberly record. The standing stones look 'like men guarding the cairn'; he has 'the odd illusion of that extra dimension into which our solid world stands back'; in his dream the bones he has discovered in the cairn become living figures; and at one point he is conscious of 'invisible traffic' between himself and the place where he has stored the bones, and feels that he is being 'influenced'. He reflects that 'The influence was obviously nothing more than his own unconscious prompting'. Obviously; but we don't altogether believe him.

These inklings, and Grant's reflections on the nature of time and its relationship with the timeless, are his own, and never take the form of direct authorial comment. And yet four answers to fundamental questions about these matters are given at different points in the book – one intellectual, one emotional, one psychological, and one practical – and each immediately invites further questions, which is entirely proper, particularly in Martin's case, when we consider the later history of concentration camp survivors. There are disturbing or refreshing images in the writing itself: the stone circle is 'little more than a ghost-hedge of modest-sized stones'; a woman looks at Grant with 'a tragic spirit-face'. There are recurring images of light and rebirth: 'the secret life in the sunlight, which was everywhere without going anywhere'; 'the western ocean... had upon its evening face a mingling of light, a curious crawling effect, like a marvelling'.

The book mixes categories – it's at once comic, tragic, beautiful, terrible, simple, poetic, and inscrutable. From its whole course and texture – rich in dramatic incident and good-humoured observation – we gain a sense that the meaning of the story is not imposed on it by the writer's art, or drawn from it by our own need, but emerges naturally and essentially for those willing to glimpse movement out of the corner of an eye. At one moment Grant has a feeling that a sudden insight 'was true in the very essence of himself, yet an essence apprehended outside himself, like the evening light'. As a matter of authentic experience this kind of apprehension 'in the very essence of oneself' is exactly the way in which truth is realized. At another point, soon after Grant has been rescued from drowning, he exclaims, 'Dear God, there's hope for the world!' *The Silver Bough* communicates powerfully that this is indeed the case.

The story as you move with it seems entirely simple and natural, producing its magic through the most direct and factual descriptions of time and place: 'The light was growing green outside and fading away in the room. Things were settling down for the night, rocks and stones and the little pathway. The fowls were silent, the cat jumped up on the garden wall...'(*SB* 87). Why, as we read, do we have the sense of waiting for something?

THE LOST CHART

The Lost Chart (1949) was written at a time when the Cold War between the Soviet Union and the West, and the threat of the atom bomb which lurked behind every dispute, however small, created an atmosphere of suspicion, tension, fear and unease. There was a culture of espionage, counter-espionage, and weird forms of clandestine sabre-rattling.

The aims of *The Lost Chart,* and the reason for the choice of the spy genre to embody them, are plain enough. At the end of the book, Dermot, very much the 'Gunn-character', reflects,

> And if in man's madness it did come to utmost violence, to lost pockets of earth with small surviving groups from world cata-strophe, then more real than ever would be the need to know how to salute the face of the God of life, bow to the white moon of the seasons, and find again what was behind the wave... (*LC* 349)

The references here are to prayers in *Carmina Gadelica,* a store of material from the old Gaelic culture collected and translated by Alexander Carmichael,[2] which is quoted several times in the text of *The Lost Chart.*

There is reference, too, in that passage, to Aunt Phemie's observation in *The Shadow* that 'men have gone mad', while efforts at the totalitarian mind-control examined in *The Green Isle* have by 1949 become common all over the world.

Something else is basic to the aims of the book. Gunn makes an astonishingly open confession through Dermot of what Gaelic culture meant to him, in language which comes dangerously close to the cadences of Fiona Macleod. In so doing he lays himself open to the critical gaze of that pale, cold face which he always imagined to be focused on his work.

> The song – and the singing – had a whole civilisation behind it, an attitude to life and death over a long time... The sea and flowers on the machair; youth and the morning. Twilight. To you also I belonged once but I never can again for I am Youth.
>
> It was all there. It had manners. It was bright and sharp, and it grew mellow in age. It was sad to a depth that no lead sounded. Beautiful it was...
>
> Say it, say it once, say it was a beautiful thing that was murdered; even though they have made you feel a fool when you are saying it, say it. Say it once to your own heart, unashamed before you grow strong again, and ordinary, and deny it. (*LC* 307)

There it is. It has been said.

Dermot, the hero of the story, is caught between the police and a communist fifth column. At a time of crisis he loses a sea chart which is of value to the 'underground' and in seeking to retrieve it finds himself spying for the authorities. The chart details the waters around Cladday, the island that symbolizes for Dermot the values of Gaelic culture. Throughout the book an uneasy ambiguity leaves a disquieting impression of some important questions left unresolved in the author's mind.

The genre does not suit him. The action is city bound, with repeated pursuits of shadows through dark streets, his old suspicion of city life resurfacing in the observation that to divorce men from the direct and ancient relationship with the natural world must lead to violence.

Dermot admits that we cannot return to earlier cultural patterns, since the individual spirit will not be repressed in its search through science and art for new visions of meaning. How then, if we manage to survive the darkness of the time, can we protect essential human values?

The plot depends so much on a series of increasingly unlikely coincidences that doubts are bound to arise in the reader's mind. More surprisingly, Dermot's conversations with Christina, the Highland girl from whom he gains most of his information, seem patronizing and inauthentic. Against the author's intention, Dermot gives the impression that self-regard has distorted his perceptions. Normally in such dialogues Gunn would be guided by intuition based on knowledge and experience, but throughout this book the language seems forced, as if, instead of being spontaneously imagined, much is invented, 'made up'.

Yet whatever weaknesses *The Lost Chart* may have, it gives Gunn the opportunity to make statements close to his heart. Cladday is 'the land of light... you can watch God painting out there'. But although God paints, 'man has to create his own drama of the light'. The book is one more venture into darkness in order to assert the supremacy of light, yet the venture is beset by doubt; since Cladday is to be fortified, has Dermot defended or betrayed it?

THE WELL AT THE WORLD'S END

In *The Lost Chart* Gunn asked himself whether humanity could survive through a time of darkness and destruction with positive values intact. *The Well at the World's End* (1951), on the contrary, seeks for light. Here is the author trying in a letter to his puzzled publisher Geoffrey Faber to explain the book:

> Where most novels of the more ambitious kind today deal with violence and materialism leading to negation and despair, I thought it might be a change if I got a character who would wander among his fellows looking for the positive aspects of life. Is it possible to pierce the negative husk, the dark cloud, even for a few moments and come on the light, the bubbling well at the end of the fairy tale? Do folk still do it, ordinary people? Can this feeling be conveyed, the moment of wonder, of integration? (*SL* 107)

Of course 'ordinary people' still have these experiences, but any effort to concentrate on them was regarded at the time as escapism. Faber had begun to look for puzzles in Gunn where none existed. The problem was that they could find no file in which to place *The Well at the World's End*. It is at once a picaresque adventure story, a modern folk tale, and a legend for the times.

Peter Munro, Professor of History, on holiday in the Highlands with his wife Fand, is haunted by the gloom of the Cold War and feels an urgent need to move through the living world and share its vitality. Peter and Fand are directed to a well to fill their kettle and find it empty – yet at a touch pure, invisible water shivers with light.

As they share the wonder of this apparent miracle, Fand tells Peter the legend of the well at the world's end, which grants to those who discover it both knowledge and poetry. In order to find the well, you have to cross a boundary between worlds, yet the novel as it unfolds tells us that the boundary once crossed, the traveller moves more deeply into the world where all of us live, but now he is awake instead of asleep. I suggest that it is important that Fand tells the story to the professor, and not the other way round.

The urge to go away on his own, to meet people by chance, grows ever stronger in Peter as he reflects that 'He would have to forget himself... forget his "importance", his notion of being "somebody". He says nothing of all this to Fand, but – "You can go any time," she said.'

The story can be read simply as a series of encounters only related by the fact that they happen to one person in sequence. But it is notable that most of them are based on actual experience – they either happened to Gunn himself or were told to him by close friends in whom he could place complete trust: the empty well which was full; the appearance of the 'wild man' on the bridge; the revelation in the Spanish garden; the strangely birdless, scentless, soundless wood; the tale of the malicious trick and the haunted house and, finally, the incident when he goes to the rescue of a lamb caught on a ledge, and escapes death through a grotesque accident. This comedy with a serious purpose would not do its job if it consisted merely of invention. Both light and darkness had to be real.

The Well at the World's End becomes a quest, a pilgrimage, a folk tale. Paradoxically, and necessarily, the search for wonder and delight is dogged by menace, danger and doubt. The incident of the haunted house, in particular, raises the question whether evil exists as a force directed at human beings from outside. The suggestion is that it does, and is given its opportunity, by negative emotion and blind will, to overwhelm the mind. The only defence against it is the experience of light as an inner reality.

The essence of the book, though, lies in the moments of illumination which occur along the way, when the mind is struck awake and sees everything anew – after a brush with death the revelation that 'there exists an order of things outside our conception of time'; the joy in the eyes of a middle-aged woman when a dance restores her sense of youth; a shepherd's confession of his sudden realization of the mystery and beauty of the world; a girl singing for the song's sake; Peter's sudden sense that 'Immediately the ego with its demands was forgotten, everything was alive naturally in its own place' (*WE* 263).

Throughout the book there is a feeling of movement, open country, fresh wind.

> The little fields, coloured with crops, the grazing cattle, a woman walking inside a wooden hoop carrying two buckets of water from a well, a man mending a roof, a boy rushing after a puppy dog, a

trundling cart. Then he did a thing which he could never have conceived of his doing before: he blessed the little community. (*WE* 262)

This is a valedictory vision; the scene has a flavour of long ago, of the time when the author himself was young.

Peter Munro finds the well, at last, in the place where it always was, and where the folk tale always knew it was, in the place where he started, the place where Fand is. The secret is deep within our own nature, and not in the shimmering distance. The novel becomes a celebration of that archetypal form of human companionship known as love.

10

The Final Adventure

BLOODHUNT

The final adventure consisted of three books: a novel which spoke entirely through story, and kept the exact balance that Gunn had long been seeking; a novel which assailed the impossible like one of those cliff climbs he describes so often; and an autobiography which isn't one.

Bloodhunt (1952) is on the face of it a story about a retired sailor living on an isolated croft, whose life is disrupted by a sudden call on all his mental and spiritual resources. But as usual it is a great deal more than that. Sandy is seen locally as a 'character' and accepts his semi-comic reputation without rancour, hoping to end his days in peace, even perhaps to discover before he goes whether 'the spirit was immortal'.

A visit from the local policeman knocks his expectations sideways. Sandy finds himself protecting Allan, a young man who has killed the policeman's brother in a fight. He would prefer to evade responsibility, and dodges examination of his motives, but one intuitive action leads to another, and he is caught in the trap which his croft becomes as the search for the fugitive intensifies.

The old sailor is forced into taxing manoeuvres and stratagems as he tries to provision Allan, the young man who has helped him so often on the farm, but he injures himself in an accident and his formidable neighbour, the widow Macleay, insists on looking after him – 'She moved about with remarkable energy as if life had been given a new meaning, and so great was her pleasure in its exercise that obstacles added an invigorating tang.' (*B* 111). The widow is a commanding presence who gives to the book the freshness of vital comedy.

Finally, Allan's girlfriend, made pregnant by the man Allan killed, arrives on the doorstep, turned out by her parents.

The novel is one of Gunn's best for several reasons: to tell the story even in bald outline would make its meaning clear, but, far from being a bald outline, it is presented with balanced economy and poetic precision. Everything depends on the reality of Sandy and it is often said that to portray a good man is the most difficult achievement in fiction. Sandy is proof that it can be done.

Gunn has said that he had in mind when writing *Bloodhunt* the situation which would be faced by isolated groups who survived atomic warfare, seeking rules by which to live. Sandy is in effect 'the old man of the tribe', making decisions which decide fate. The story examines the effect on such a man and his community of intrusion by violence and negative emotion. Sandy is faced with the problem of how to help Allan without condoning the crime, and how finally to break out of the malign cycle of murder and revenge as the policeman's pursuit grows increasingly personal and vindictive.

The virus of negative emotion spreads through the community. The policeman's mother drives him deeper into black obsession. The parents of the pregnant girl repudiate her. Everywhere there is dark rumour about Allan's whereabouts.

Sandy has an ongoing dispute with the minister, who is impatient with his friend's personal philosophy, contending that only the doctrine and discipline of the Church can maintain the human community. When he complains to Sandy about the violence in contemporary films, 'if they must have fear in their picture houses...give them the fear of God', Sandy replies, 'Either that or the love of Christ' (*B* 191).

Ironically, when Sandy seems on the way to the Styx after his accident, and the minister insists on praying at his bedside, he ends his prayer with the words 'I bring you this new commandment: love one another'. Left later to face his problems in the dark, Sandy reflects, 'We don't want to love one another...Words! Words! I only want to be left alone.' (*B* 195).

This brings Gunn's attitude to Christianity into sharp focus. He was unimpressed by dogma of any kind, and by institutional limits placed on individual discovery, but his respect and affection for the life and teachings of Jesus is made clear as early as *Sun Circle*. At one point in *Bloodhunt* this comment occurs: 'Of all the stories man had made only two were immortal: the story of Cain and the story of Christ.' (*B* 233).

Gunn had a profound concern with the mystery that is life, and a strong sense of something unspecified which lies behind it. 'Mystery. That was the last word...', but 'In a moment of freedom he [Sandy] saw life and the world as a blessed gift and stood at the heart of what seemed the creative intention.' (*B* 209).

Sandy's conduct is governed by a continual awareness both of the needs of his tribe and his own communion with 'the tap-roots of life'. So in the end, when he sees Allan and the policeman Nicol fighting to the death, and finds Allan's body, he buries it and decides that 'he would say nothing... to anyone'. 'In all conscience, there had been enough violence and his mind called halt.' (*B* 248).

Violence, revenge, vendetta have been the curse of many cultures; civilization has merely disguised it.

THE OTHER LANDSCAPE

The story of *Bloodhunt* perfectly embodies its meaning. In *The Other Landscape* (1954), by contrast, Gunn takes the risk of allowing characters to explore his meaning in words that go beyond words. A novel about the inner nature of God must be a raid on the impossible.

The narrator, Urquhart, travels to the Highlands to seek out the writer of a piece of visionary prose which describes shipwreck and death on a night of storm. The first shock for Urquhart is to discover that the author, Douglas Menzies, lost his wife in childbirth during just such a storm; the second shock is to discover that the writing was not an act of retrospect but of prescience. Menzies is a musician who now lives as a recluse, set on a quest to discover the nature of the reality into which Annabel has disappeared, and so confront the cosmic Wrecker who destroyed her.

This is the only novel in which Gunn employs a first-person narrator, a device which proves oddly liberating. Instead of identifying with a 'Gunn-character' he uses Urquhart as an unreliable observer, subject to confusion and misunderstanding, who must learn as he goes.

The book juggles various themes, each distinctive in weight, mood and atmosphere. Menzies' quest is treated throughout with intense and concentrated seriousness; yet the love story of Urquhart and Catherine, the girl he meets in the hotel – so beautiful, understanding and intelligent as to be wildly unlikely in any circumstances – is in effect a comedy romance; while the tale of the nihilistic Major (resurrected from Colonel Hicks in *The Lost Glen*) who tyrannizes over the hotel staff, darts continually from bouts of devious metaphysical argument to scenes of drama or wild farce.

Themes and events mirror and distort one another. We are forced into radical questioning of the nature of time, into ambiguities of second sight and survival after death, and into 'recurrence', when patterns of events inexplicably repeat themselves.

Urquhart finds that time past and time present merge, that situations change shape and meaning, that he continually misunderstands Menzies, Catherine and their relationship, that the Major practises deliberate deception out of a bitter contempt for life in all its manifestations. Finally, the community's revenge on the Major (and Gunn's revenge on the figure who gave rise to his portrait of Hicks in *The Lost Glen*) takes the form of a surreal accident. The Major is doused with water from a hose-pipe as a self-created fire in his room is extinguished by his 'innocent' gillie. Nothing, in other words, is what it seems. Urquhart steps daily from the shifting comedy of guests in a fishing hotel to stark tragedy of sea and storm, and the ruthless isolation of the dedicated Menzies.

Menzies tells Urquhart during their first highly metaphysical conversation that 'the Wrecker is God when he wrecks', and that

> God's ways are non-rational, either non-rational or there is no God. Were it otherwise, did God exist and were he rational, then his doings would be susceptible of a logical exposition. His horrors wouldn't call for faith. So if there is a God – he must have a different system. (*OL* 70)

We are being asked to explore this 'different system', which must by definition be invisible to human eyes because we are part of it.

The freshly growing love of Catherine and Urquhart – through which Urquhart blunders with a clumsiness which no 'Gunn-character' would display – relates to the profound and intense relationship of Menzies and his wife Annabel, a relationship that persists for Menzies long after her death. We are being asked to accept that the relationship of Catherine and Urquhart may develop into something as significant as that of their mentors. In the same hall of mirrors we can see Menzies' pursuit of the landscape beyond the Wrecker as reflected in the Major's search for a congenial hell in which to endure his life.

Not only do the intertwining stories form a network of prevision, recurrence and ambiguity, but the text contains a series of symbols which arouse further questions. Menzies rescues a cask from the sea after the storm. The cask contains rum (spirit) and the rum sustains Menzies in the months that follow Annabel's death – not merely the drink itself but the need to climb down the cliff to fetch it. When Urquhart inspects the cask after Menzies' own death, he finds it empty.

Similarly, Menzies' only companion, the savage black dog (misfortune) which guards the house, goes over the cliff onto the rocks after its master, leaving a smell of brimstone on the air. The dog has made its final statement by knocking over a candle, so burning down the house and destroying Menzies' music.

Ideas proliferate in the book: about the relationship between physics, metaphysics and the psyche; about the Wrecker as an aspect of God; about the fundamental value of the creative process, and its association with the love between human beings; about the existence of that 'other landscape' which lies beyond the Wrecker's reach.

The Wrecker enters, at the level of human perception, from experience, where plans, theories, relationships, hopes, cultures, ways of life can be destroyed suddenly by illness, accident and events so arbitrary as to appear meaningless, or so persistent as to seem malign. The Greeks understood that to congratulate yourself on good fortune or success is to invite disaster, as if this were a law rather than a mere superstition. I do not think that Gunn intends to imply a force which intervenes in specific lives at particular times, but a malignity which lies at the heart of reality, making such events possible. It is as if creation were itself a propulsion from inner conflict, leaving humanity to distinguish aspects of the spiritual world, and so fight through to an understanding which enables the positive to hold its own. Menzies' search, then, is more than a search for the dead Annabel, it is 'a sort of warfare in those regions which the Wrecker inhabits'.

In the realm of the Wrecker, suffering is increased by the sense of guilt. Religion loads us with guilt even before we have the opportunity to perform acts which would warrant it, through the malign doctrine of 'original sin'. But if there is such guilt at the heart of Creation, it is the Wrecker's guilt.

Menzies' release is shared by Urquhart in a vision:

> his expression deepened in recognition, as if a beloved woman had entered the room ... the compulsion to turn, to follow his eyes, is too strong for the cramped reluctance that would defeat it. So I turn round and see Annabel standing in the doorway...
>
> ...the whole energy of her being is in her eyes. And her eyes recognise Menzies with an intensity that is tragic and beautiful... This terrible living quality, this sheer expression of love at its ultimate moment of wordless communion becomes unbearable, and I stir and get up, perhaps, God knows, to make way for her. The movement brings a dizziness to my head, a momentary half-darkness, and the door is empty. (*OT* 242)

At this moment the dead Annabel is more real than the living Catherine in whom we are also asked to believe. The expression on Annabel's face, Urquhart eventually realizes, is the look with which she bade farewell to Menzies on the night of storm. Whatever the 'explanation' for the vision – and several are proposed – it frees Menzies from the oppression of the Wrecker. It cannot free him from the Wrecker himself – as events immediately demonstrate. But liberation enables him to write music again – music which 'the Wrecker' destroys.

The 'presence' of Annabel was not a return from the dead to bring comfort but a living vision, a recognition of the power of human love and its ability to pierce the unreality of time. Menzies, Urquhart says, 'was bigger than the Wrecker. And what made him bigger was love, because love was ... the creative element that made his music' (*OL* 258). The darkness is real, but 'Against that darkness man has the light, the warmth, the other insight which love has fashioned for him ... on the eternal quest' (*OL* 307).

At the end everything tangible which Menzies has created has vanished. What does this mean? That there is a level on which understanding has value whether or not it can be communicated to others. It is part of the inexhaustible creative force which lies beyond the power of the Wrecker but which can only be reached through inner work, by following insight and experience from one milestone to another. Gunn records both in *The Well at the World's End* and *The Atom of Delight* his awakening in a Spanish garden after a brush with death: 'the stillness itself was holding something...what it was holding was time', and 'there exists an order of things outside our conception of time'.

Through most of the book, Urquhart has been moving in a state of bewilderment, tossing in his sleep, but at one moment and another moment, moments out of time, he is awake – 'The innocence of the morning. The freshness. The forgotten, the secret landscape...'.

When he finds Menzies' body at the bottom of the cliff, 'the expression was hardly a smile but rather a characteristic or veiled intensity arrested in quietude...from having heard the struck note and knowing what the note meant' (*OL* 314). Perhaps it meant that we can rely on the spiritual reality of light.

Gunn's own resolution in the face of the Wrecker was soon to be tested. The love between himself and his wife Daisy had been the inspiration for faith in that of Annabel and Menzies. She died nine years after the publication of the book. Recurrence. He was forced to embark on his own journey through darkness and loneliness. His whole work can be seen as a series of efforts to make the perception of a double landscape real to his readers.

The novel is flawed and difficult. Menzies is convincing as a proposition, a psychological situation, but not entirely as a human being. The language in the conversations that are basic to the story is so elliptical and abstruse as to evade immediate understanding. And while the language of the story itself is fresh, vigorous and visually invigorating, it can be problematic. Here is Urquhart gazing at the sky: 'The blue was high and serene and its dream began in the stillness that lies beyond the last thought.' This is highly impressionistic. It was not the sky but Urquhart who was dreaming and went beyond the dream. The meaning therefore is that a mind contemplating the blueness of blue and the skyness of sky can move beyond thought to an inner stillness which illuminates – what? The nature of reality, or something 'beyond' reality? Urquhart, anyway, realizes that 'there may be an order of being to which delight is natural'. Significantly, Gunn's last book was called *The Atom of Delight*.

I suggest that we are not in fact searching literature for 'the perfect novel'. The value of the novel is that it is capable of anything – poetry, philosophy, psychology, and above all the illumination of life. Literature depends for its vitality on exploration, on the discoveries made and the surprises encountered on the way. In folk tales it is the wanderer who goes aside to help the old woman or to mend the raven's wing who reaches the well at the world's end. We need stories which move and challenge mind and spirit, which spring out on us, which break open mind and make us recognize what we always knew but had forgotten. As Gunn puts it in the book, 'What had been unthinkable is in a moment apprehended.' (OL 306). If the story of *The Other Landscape* is followed with patience we do indeed gain the sense of seeing things as if for the first time.

THE ATOM OF DELIGHT

For some years before *Bloodhunt* restored their faith Faber had viewed Gunn's novels with some misgivings – why not another *Morning Tide* or another *Silver Darlings*? – and Gunn felt the strain. When *The Other Landscape* failed both commercially and critically, fiction-seeds ceased to grow in his mind.

In *The Other Landscape* he had explored the heart of darkness. To rediscover and establish the reality of light, he had to base himself firmly on experience, for, as he wrote on the third page of his last book,

> Clearly in the pursuit of the atom of delight autobiography must provide the atom. Any other way of providing it would be an imagined way. That might save the face of the self but the self could never then say: It happened to me. (*AD* 9)

But *The Atom of Delight* (1956) is autobiography only in the sense that it presents episodes from the life as focus points. Autobiography becomes the ground from which the flight takes off, and the book might be better described as reflective philosophy. In the middle of composing the textual arabesques, he dashed off a letter:

> But assuming the thing will have a shape it will be an autobio-graphy, a detective story, a Freudian analysis (of Freud), a spoon for physics, a critical commentary on Yeats, Proust, Wordsworth, Rilke, and Uncle Tom Eliot, a high dive and a long swim into anthropology, poaching, church attendance, and sucking eggs, and a way of using these and much more in a sustained, convoluting, forward-and-backward search, with a ruthless precision in the complexities of expression, into the nature of Delight... I shan't be surprised if its half-concealed logic works up into a simple, naive philosophic system... Though I'll do my best with camouflage. (*SL* 123)

It's worth looking carefully into this account. He talks of a 'ruthless precision in the complexities of expression', yet the book is often accused by readers of being vague, difficult and evasive. There is indeed much that is evasive, much that is difficult, and much that is elusive in the text, but nothing that is vague. An examination, for example, of the drastic limitation of human nature in the doctrines of behaviourism ends with the phrase 'Pavlov did not succeed in producing the gayest of dogs', which not only sums up the argument but opens the mind to the possibility that joy may be as close to the essence of life as is salivation at the prospect of food.

Again, a formal philosopher could not improve upon 'If life-mind is a function of matter then it would seem that the capacity of matter to function in this way must be latent within it', while it does not need a philosopher to appreciate the exactness of this description: 'The sea was so full that it sighed. On the other side of the harbour entrance the small waves ran along the wooden piles of the breakwater, lipping them; and beyond, on the shingly beach, it broke in a small edging of white lace that shone before the bubbles died.' (*AD* 107). He is justified in claiming precision of utterance. Indeed, the book is, among other things, an exercise in carefully meditated style.

The problem is not that he is too vague but, on the contrary, that he is attempting to be precise about perceptions and experiences that are subtle and elusive in themselves – as difficult as describing colours to a blind man – so that the following mind may get lost and fail to regain the path.

The short story which he 'plants in the middle' is a fresh and detailed account of the boy's struggle to catch a salmon bare-handed, another version of which appears in *Highland River*. Such incidents recur in novel after novel because he can rely on them as valid in experience. Now he must claim them as his own. Of course the story as told in *The Atom* is as much fiction as the story as told in *Highland River* because to recreate an incident from memory is to imagine it. The difference lies in the overt claim 'This is what happened'.

'I shouldn't be surprised if its half-concealed logic works up into a simple, naive philosophic system...Though I'll do my best with camouflage.' That is accurate enough. The argument does in fact work itself up into a not-so-simple and far-from-naive philosophic view, tied closely to the experiences on which it is based, and entirely free from jargon – though not from insights and implications as slippery and difficult to catch as any salmon. Then why the camouflage? Because to lay claim to a system would be to invite the kind of destructive analysis which it is the mission of the book to make irrelevant, and because he takes a positive pleasure in being evasive. Indeed, it has become a way of life. It is obvious throughout that he does not in fact regard the 'philosophic system' as in any way naive.

You learn less about the emotional problems of Neil Miller Gunn from *The Atom of Delight* than from any one of the novels. Evasiveness produces serious peculiarities in the way the story is told. The fact that the central figure – who is, after all, the author himself – is referred to as 'the boy' gives the account an oddly generalized air, and occasionally arouses an uneasy sense that 'the boy' is being approved of in a way which would be unlikely if the author were directly approving of Neil Gunn. The method leads to strange circumlocutions, too: 'Will worked in the Admiralty and the other in the Home Office'. It takes us a few moments to realize that this 'other' is the author wearing a disguise. The third person is itself protective cover which prevents the hunter from becoming the hunted.

Gunn was a warm, courteous man, full of humour and wisdom, who was interested in the views and experience of others, and patient with the unresponsive, but who could withdraw into cold detachment if a persistent stranger crossed invisible boundaries. His feelings were passionate and went deep, as the novels show, but to address the reader directly was not in his nature. Remembering this we still have to ask, Is it legitimate to present your life as a subject for reflection if you are not prepared to give it whole, to show us the mean, vain and murky moments along with the joyful ones; in other words if you are not prepared to 'give yourself away'? All he will say about his early life in London that is expressly confessional is: 'there were dreary spells as dreary as the streets, anxieties and frets and miseries and fears and conflicts and temptations and illicit desires and obsessive sex and the rest' (*AD* 215–16). Nothing here is made explicit, nothing brought alive. What darkness there is in the book is almost metaphysical – the boy's fear of the formless night, and attack on the man by a force like 'black electricity'.

But then we have to accept the explicit intention of *The Atom of Delight*, which is to show where light is to be found in the life of a particular boy at a particular time, for when light is found it becomes possible to accept the dark. To Gunn the source of delight lies in the realization of a 'second self' which comes into its own when the everyday self, the willing ego, is momentarily bypassed or forgotten – as in the phrase 'he raced so fast that he left himself behind'. Only when it is understood that this hidden self is real and permanent can freedom become possible and shame, mistrust and humiliation fall into place. He writes: 'The second self is not an assumption. It is the fount from which assumptions proceed.'

Throughout the book – and in most of the later novels – we gain a feeling that the more exact our observation of this world, the more strongly the suspicion arises that other dimensions exist and that paradoxes of time and physics form a unity. This argument – if that's what it is – rests on delight as a creative experience, and develops its own logic. We have forgotten what we know and must rediscover it.

Gunn said once, 'When I finished 'The Atom of Delight' I felt that was the end of my youth and now I'd really get down to it... But the energy wasn't there. You need to be able to concentrate and I couldn't manage it.'

The Atom of Delight was almost totally ignored on publication and sold poorly, for readers who read Gunn for the story could not find one and were disappointed. Yet it was a comfort to him in the years that followed that letters of appreciation arrived from individuals of many kinds in many places, demonstrating that it is one of those books about which a man here and a woman there feels immediately 'It was written for me', returning to them a secret which they had always known but inexplicably lost.

11

Postscript

We have come a long way from the account of Neil Gunn as a writer 'at his best when describing the ordinary life and background of a crofting community and when he interprets in simple prose the complex character of the Celt'. Gunn was himself a complex character, whether or not he could be defined as a Celt, and one capable of a vital and refreshing simplicity. But he did not set out merely to describe in simple prose the life and background of a crofting community. He wrote in order to make a living, to rid himself of frustrations, and to get at the truth about a world which is not a simple place.

Living in the Highlands did not make him 'provincial' in any sense. He was fully aware of the movements in world literature, and of the political and social developments which endangered civilization itself. Distance from the urban illusion of control over affairs seemed to add clarity to the view.

Not only was he involved with the Scottish literary renaissance, and at one time or another friendly with Hugh MacDiarmid, Edwin Muir, James Bridie, Eric Linklater, Naomi Mitchison, George Blake and many others, but he read widely among the modernists, mentioning in *The Atom of Delight* Proust, Yeats, Rilke, Eliot, Robert Graves, Lawrence, as well as thinkers such as J. G. Frazer, Freud, Jung, Lao Tzu, and the Zen Buddhists (in whom he became particularly interested), as well as a number of Western philosophers and several physicists. But he also makes use of folk tale, myth, legend, and celebrates the ancient culture of his own people with its unique store of music, song, and story.

It could be said that there is technical modernism in *Highland River*, *The Key of the Chest*, *The Shadow* and *The Other Landscape*, which proves only that he was neither traditionalist nor deliberate innovator, but sought a personal solution to problems of every kind at every level.

The writers he found most companionable (a favourite word) were not as a rule the most fashionable at the time, but individualists like himself – the sly, anarchistic maverick John Cowper Powys; the profound and sardonic Icelander Halldor Laxness; the highly philosophical L. H. Myers; the English traditional novelist R. C. Hutchinson; the poets Norman MacCaig, Edwin Muir and Stewart Conn; R. H. Blyth's translations of haiku, and so on.

He was unwilling to admit a vocation for literature, and avoided any claim to be 'a writer' until he had achieved a measure of success. Indeed, he remained evasive about his degree of commitment, writing to Nan Shepherd, 'I am not really a literary man...For I don't know that one ever wants to have an understanding with anything so much as with life.' (*SL* 13). This meant, I think, that he did not want to live in a closed occupational world, that he was not interested in artistic squabbles, that writing was not entered into for critical applause and renown but as a medium for exploring life's texture, value and significance.

When induced to discuss the themes and intentions of his work, he usually led the way into accounts of crucial personal experiences and their meaning, and so into realms of philosophical implication. He spent as much time as he could out of doors walking, fishing and watching the natural world going about its business.

Close attention to his writing will show that the more exactly he observes the living reality before his eyes, the more an intimation of 'something other' is communicated. Birds, beasts, flowers, fish, people, the movements of sea and weather come alight on the page, so that a dog able to read might ask itself, 'How does he know all this?' The answer lies in an ancient saying quoted in a book, *Zen Flesh, Zen Bones*, which lay at his bedside during his last months, 'Look lovingly on some object. Do not go on to another object. Here, in the middle of the object – the blessing.'[1] The result is to arouse in the reader a sense of wonder at the whole network of factual astonishments which comprise the world.

He said once that, if he had acquired sufficient money early enough to finance the adventure, he would have enjoyed a career as a gambler, and the first page he turned to on receipt of his daily *Scotsman* was the financial page to check share prices. But this aspiration fell into the same half-jocular category as his repeated threat to buy a Jaguar – from which extravagance he had to be restrained because by this time his eyesight made him a menace to traffic.

Paradoxically, although he preferred to see himself as an intuitive writer, he was proud of his ability as a craftsman, and praised James Bridie's insistence that writing is first and foremost a craftsman's job. His own advice to younger writers was technical, practical and acute, delivered with tact and patience.

He often referred approvingly to Gurdjieff's[2] dictum that no one could start on the path to wisdom until he had established himself as a 'householder', which did not mean a property owner, but an individual with the ability to conduct practical and emotional affairs with competence and assurance. In this sense Gunn was a householder in literature as well as in life.

The seriousness of his engagement with writing is shown clearly by every book he produced. The claim to a measure of detachment was not an example of evasion. The ability to take a full part in life yet remain an observer is necessary to inner growth. The ego operates, the second self is witness. Writing for Gunn became a pilgrimage, a form of inner work. He knew well enough that the more difficult and experimental his books were, the less he would be appreciated. He persisted because he had an urge to explore and to communicate. Although he needed to earn a living, what was fundamentally important in the end was the necessity to continue this inner work and to give it authentic expression in art. It seems to me high time that Gunn was accepted as what he is, a writer of European stature.

Notes

CHAPTER 1. LIFE AND BACKGROUND

1. C. M. Grieve (Hugh MacDiarmid) (1892–1978). MacDiarmid's early
   lyrics in Scots, together with the long poem *A Drunk Man Looks at the
   Thistle*, fired Scottish poetry into the era of literary modernism. A
   firebrand with a prodigious talent for controversy and another for
   turning political and intellectual somersaults, he regarded Gunn as
   a comrade during the 1920s, but the two men fell out when
   MacDiarmid dismissed Gunn in cavalier fashion as 'a writer of the
   '90s' and announced that novels were of no importance for Scotland
   when compared with poetry. This did not prevent Gunn from
   participating in the effort to gain for the poet a Civil List pension.
2. Francis Russell Hart (1927–2001), Professor of English at the
   University of Massachusetts, Boston, published in 1963 a penetrating article on three Gunn novels, entitled 'Neil Gunn's Fiction of
   Violence', and later devoted special attention to Gunn in his
   ground-breaking book *The Scottish Novel*. The two men became
   friends; Gunn valued him highly both as man and critic.
3. Thomas Henry Huxley (1825–95), naturalist, zoologist and brilliant
   lecturer on science, became a combative champion of Darwin's
   theories of evolution.
4. Ernst Haeckel (1834–1919), Professor at Jena Zoological Institute,
   and author of *The Riddle of the Universe* (1899), which applied
   Darwin's theories to philosophy and religion, concluding that there
   is no personal God, no immortal soul and no free will.
5. Henry George (1839–1907), American political economist, whose
   Progress and Poverty (1879) argued that State revenue should be
   raised by a single tax on land-rent.
6. Walter Pater (1839–94), aesthete, stylist and advocate of 'Art for Art's
   sake'.
7. Maurice Walsh became a popular writer of outdoor romance. He
   had difficulties with plot, and Gunn supplied him with ideas on

request. Gunn appears, disguised as an Irishman and under the pseudonym Neil Quinn in *The Key Above the Door* (1926).

8. Tom Johnston (1881–1965), radical Labour MP, was appointed Secretary of State for Scotland in Churchill's wartime government. He set up a Scottish Council of State, and established the North of Scotland Hydro-Electric Board, which proved to be a major contribution to the regeneration of the Highlands.

9. John McCormick (1904–61) was a Glasgow lawyer who as a student became a founder member of the National Party of Scotland, and, after the amalgamation of this group with the Scottish Party, Secretary to the SNP. In 1942 he resigned when the SNP split over support for the war effort, and helped to establish the Scottish Convention, which collected some two million signatures on a petition requesting the establishment of a Scottish parliament.

10. Gunn's anarchism was based on Peter Kropotkin's theory of mutual aid within species, which Kropotkin wrote as a counter to the extreme social Darwinism of 'nature red in tooth and claw'. The form of mutual aid practised in Highland crofting communities when Gunn was a boy is described in *The Serpent*, pp. 197–200. See Peter Kropotkin. *Mutual Aid: A Factor in Evolution* (London: William Heinemann, 1902), and Peter Kropotkin *Memoirs of a Revolutionist* (London: Folio Society, 1978).

CHAPTER 6. CASTING ABOUT

1. Nan Shepherd (1893–1981) was for over forty years a lecturer in English at what became the Aberdeen College of Education. She was a writer of emotional depth and sensitivity, whose novels, *The Quarry Wood* (1928), *The Weatherhouse* (1930) and *A Pass in the Grampians* (1933) had been generally forgotten until reissued in the Canongate Classics series, now available in one volume (1996).

2. James Bridie was the pseudonym of physician O. H. Mavor (1888–1951), one of Scotland's most talented and successful playwrights, founder of the Glasgow Citizens' Theatre and a man Gunn admired for his practical and forthright benevolence. Their epistolary skirmishes were always good-humoured; Bridie was able to make criticisms which would have been found offensive if offered by anyone else.

3. J. W. Dunne (1875–1949). His book *An Experiment with Time* (1927), propounding a theory of time as the fourth dimension, had a vogue in the 1930s, causing many devotees to record their dreams in order to discover whether they related to future as well as past events.

CHAPTER 7. *YOUNG ART AND OLD HECTOR* AND *THE GREEN ISLE OF THE GREAT DEEP*

1. William Blake, *Auguries of Innocence*.

CHAPTER 9. EXPLORATIONS

1. See *Selected Letters of Edwin Muir*, ed. P. H. Butter. (Edinburgh; London: Hogarth Press, 1974), p. 150.
2. An excellent paperback edition of *Carmina Gadelica* was issued by Loris Books (Edinburgh) in 1992.

CHAPTER 11. POSTSCRIPT

1. *Zen Flesh, Zen Bones*, compiled by Paul Reps (New York: Charles E. Tuttle 1957; London: Penguin Books, 1971).
2. G. I. Gurdjieff (1866–1949). Controversial guru first encountered by Gunn in P. D. Ouspensky's account of his teaching, *In Search of the Miraculous* (London: Routledge, 1950). Gunn's interest was aroused by Gurdjieff's penetrating psychological insights, which can be tested in practice, and which correspond at some points to his own experience of 'the second self'. The cosmological material he regarded as interesting, but baffling and unnecessary. See also: James Moore's biography *Gurdjieff: The Anatomy of a Myth* (Shaftesbury: Element, 1991).

Select Bibliography

WORKS BY NEIL GUNN

The Grey Coast (London: Jonathan Cape, 1926).

Hidden Doors (short stories) (Edinburgh: Porpoise Press, 1929).

Morning Tide (Edinburgh: Porpoise Press, 1931).

Back Home: A Play in One Act, Scottish National Play Series, 9 (Glasgow: W. Wilson, 1932).

The Lost Glen (Edinburgh: Porpoise Press, 1932).

Sun Circle (Edinburgh: Porpoise Press, 1933).

Butcher's Broom (Edinburgh: Porpoise Press, 1934).

Whisky and Scotland: A Practical and Spiritual Survey (London: Routledge, 1935).

Highland River (Edinburgh: Porpoise Press, 1937).

Choosing a Play (one-act play) (Edinburgh: Porpoise Press, 1938).

Off in a Boat (London: Faber & Faber, 1938).

Old Music (one-act play), Nelson's Plays for Amateurs 2 (London: Nelson, 1939).

Net Results, Nelson's Plays for Amateurs, 11 (London: Nelson, 1939).

Wild Geese Overhead (London: Faber & Faber, 1939).

Second Sight (London: Faber & Faber, 1940).

The Silver Darlings (London: Faber & Faber, 1941).

Young Art and Old Hector (London: Faber & Faber, 1942).

Storm and Precipice, and Other Pieces (selected extracts) (London: Faber & Faber, 1942).

The Serpent (London: Faber & Faber, 1943).

The Green Isle of the Great Deep (London: Faber & Faber, 1944).

The Key of the Chest (London: Faber & Faber, 1945).

The Drinking Well (London: Faber & Faber, 1946).

The Shadow (London: Faber & Faber, 1948).

The Silver Bough (London: Faber & Faber, 1948).

The Lost Chart (London: Faber & Faber, 1949).

Highland Pack, with drawings by Keith Henderson (London: Faber & Faber, 1949).

The White Hour, and Other Stories (London: Faber & Faber, 1950).

The Well at the World's End (London: Faber & Faber, 1951).

Bloodhunt (London: Faber & Faber, 1952).

The Other Landscape (London: Faber & Faber, 1954).

The Atom of Delight (autobiography) (London: Faber & Faber, 1956).

Posthumous collections

McCulloch, Margery (ed.) *The Man Who Came Back* (Edinburgh: Polygon, 1991). A gathering of lesser Gunn essays, together with short stories, some of which were used by him as the basis for novels.

McLeery, Alistair (ed.) *Landscape and Light* (Aberdeen: Aberdeen University Press, 1991). A valuable collection of Gunn's essays collected from a variety of periodical sources.

Pick, J. B. (ed.), *Neil M. Gunn: Selected Letters*, compiled and introduced by J. B. Pick (Edinburgh: Polygon, 1987).

BOOKS ON NEIL GUNN

Burns, John, *A Celebration of the Light: Zen in the Novels of Neil M. Gunn* (Edinburgh: Canongate, 1988). Early in the 1950s Gunn recognized in Zen many of the insights which had informed his own work from the beginning. By exploring these insights, John Burns illuminates Gunn's fundamental aims.

Chapman Special Issue, ed. Joy Hendry (Edinburgh: Chapman no. 67, Winter 1991–2). Essays on the occasion of the Gunn centenary.

Gifford, Douglas, *Neil M. Gunn and Lewis Grassic Gibbon* (Edinburgh: Oliver and Boyd, 1983). A revealing comparison of two major Scottish novelists, with particular reference to Gunn's *The Silver Darlings* and Gibbon's *Scots Quair*. Gifford is a sympathetic and reliable guide, with a broad and balanced view of the Scottish tradition in literature.

Gunn, Dairmid and Isobel Murray (eds.), *Neil Gunn's Country: Essays in Celebration of Neil Gunn* (Edinburgh: Chambers, 1991). The essays are by writers who knew Gunn personally, and deal with both the land of social reality and the country of myth and symbol.

Hart, Francis Russell and J. B. Pick, *Neil M. Gunn: A Highland Life* (London: John Murray, 1981). The first full biography of Gunn.

Herbert, W. N., and Richard Price (eds.), *The Anarchy of Light: Neil Gunn – a Celebration* (Dundee: Gairfish, 1991). Essays on the occasion of the Gunn centenary.

McCulloch, Margery, *The Novels of Neil M. Gunn: A Critical Study* (Edinburgh: Scottish Academic Press, 1987). A critical examination which acts as a counterbalance to more celebratory accounts.

Morrison, David (ed.), *Essays on Neil Gunn* (Thurso: Humphries, 1971). Contains a valuable article by Francis Russell Hart.

Price, Richard, *The Fabulous Matter of Fact: The Poetics of Neil M. Gunn* (Edinburgh: Edinburgh University Press, 1991). An astute and thorough exploration of the novels, relating them both to the Scottish twentieth-century literary renaissance and to the modernist movement in European literature.

Scott, Alexander and Douglas Gifford (eds.), *Neil M. Gunn: The Man and the Writer* (Edinburgh: Blackwood, 1973). Twenty varied and informative essays comprising the first detailed study of Gunn's life and work.

Stokoe, C. J. L., *A Bibliography of the Works of Neil M. Gunn* (Aberdeen: Aberdeen University Press, 1987).

CHAPTERS AND EXTENDED PASSAGES IN GENERAL BOOKS

Bold, Alan, 'In Search of the Symbol – Neil Gunn', in Bold, *Modern Scottish Literature* (London: Longmans, 1983).

Bruce, George, 'Neil Miller Gunn', in Bruce, *Two Essays* (Edinburgh: National Library of Scotland, 1971).

Craig, Cairns, *The Modern Scottish Novel: Narrative and the National Imagination* (Edinburgh: Edinburgh University Press, 1999).

D'Arcy, Julian, *Scottish Skalds and Sagamen: Old Norse Influence on Modern Scottish Literature* (East Linton: Tuckwell Press, 1996). D'Arcy includes a chapter on Gunn, his stance shown by the statement on *Sun Circle*: 'There is simply too much myth and legend and not enough convincing historical reality.'

Crawford, Thomas, 'Region and Nation in The Silver Darlings' (Gunn) and 'The Scots Quair' (Gibbon), in R. Draper (ed.), *The Literature of Region and Nation* (London: Macmillan, 1989).

Grieve, C. M. (Hugh MacDiarmid), *Contemporary Scottish Studies*. First Series (London: Parsons, 1926). The first influential recognition of Gunn's promise and significance.

Hart, Francis Russell, *The Scottish Novel: A Critical Survey from from Smollett to Spark* (Cambridge, Mass.: Harvard University Press, 1978; London: John Murray, 1979). A monumental study which gives particular prominence to Gunn.

Hart, Francis Russell, in Cairns Craig (ed.), *History of Scottish Literature*, vol. 4, *Twentieth Century*, (Aberdeen: Aberdeen University Press, 1988). A chapter on Gunn.

Lindsay, Maurice, *History of Scottish Literature* (London: Robert Hale, 1971). Lindsay gives high praise to *The Silver Darlings* but concludes that Gunn's later interest in Zen and Gurdjieff 'blurred his practical sense of purpose', and refers to his 'retreat into a personal mysticism' – a clear example of the enduring split in Gunn criticism between those who appreciate the later novels and those who don't.

Macdonald, Angus, 'Modern Scottish Novelists', in H. J. C. Grierson (ed.), *Essays on Scottish Literature* (Edinburgh: Edinburgh University Press, 1948).

Manlove, Colin, *Scottish Fantasy Literature: A Critical Survey* (Edinburgh: Canongate Academic, 1994.) Contains an essay on *The Green Isle of the Great Deep*.

Murray, Isobel, and Bob Tait, *Ten Modern Scottish Novels* (Aberdeen: Aberdeen University Press, 1984). Contains an essay on Gunn's *The Silver Darlings*.

Pick, J. B., *The Great Shadow House: Essays on the Metaphysical Tradition in Scottish Literature* (Edinburgh: Polygon, 1993). Contains two chapters on Gunn.

Walker, Marshall, *Scottish Literature Since 1707* (London: Longman 1996). Accuses Gunn of 'ruralism' and a 'propulsion towards self-consciousness'.

G. J. Watson, 'The Novels of Neil Gunn', in David Hewitt and Michael Spiller (eds.), *Literature of the North* (Aberdeen: Aberdeen University Press, 1983).

Watson, Roderick, *The Literature of Scotland* (London: Macmillan, 1984). Contains a sympathetic and perceptive account of Gunn, paying particular attention to the technical modernism of *Highland River*.

Whyte, Christopher (ed.), *Gendering the Nation* (Edinburgh: Edinburgh University Press, 1995). Whyte's own essay, 'Fishy Masculinities: Neil Gunn's "The Silver Darlings"' is a forthright and entertaining attack on Gunn for, among other things, not knowing Gaelic, for sex scenes which resemble 'those in women's magazines', and for presenting archetypes which are 'static, transhistorical and prescriptive'.

Wittig, Kurt, *The Scottish Tradition in Literature* (Edinburgh: Oliver and Boyd, 1958). A pioneering and seminal book in which Wittig claims that 'modern Scottish literature reaches its highest peak in the novels of Neil Gunn'.

108

SELECTED ARTICLES IN NEWSPAPERS AND JOURNALS

Aitken W. R., 'Neil Gunn's Revision of His First Novel', *Bibliotek*, 6 (1971–3).

Angus, Stewart, 'The Novels of Neil Gunn', *Scottish Periodical*, vol. 1, no. 2 (Summer 1948).

Bold, Alan, 'Grey Aspects of Neil Gunn', *Glasgow Herald Weekender* (18 May 1991). This contribution to the 1991 centenary dismisses Gunn with the assertion that he is 'content to scratch at the surface of reality, scrawling sentences that rarely extend him artistically'. As literary criticism this is so wide of the mark that one can only take it as an expression of outright hostility to Gunn's tone, character and approach. There is indeed some electric charge in the novels which proves emotionally and intellectually positive for some readers and negative for others.

Burns, John, 'Neil Gunn's Other Landscape', *Chapman*, 45 (Summer 1985).

_____ 'A Meditation on Neil Gunn', *Books in Scotland*, no. 12 (May 1972).

Caird, James B., 'Gaelic Elements in the Work of Neil Gunn', *Studies in Scottish Literature*, 15 (1980).

_____ 'Neil Gunn, The Man and His Work', *Scotsman*, 27 September 1975.

Gifford, Douglas, 'Neil Gunn's Fiction of Delight', *Scottish International Review*, May 1972.

Graeme, Alan, 'The Modern Novelist and the Scottish Highlands: Neil Gunn's Accomplishment', *Scots Magazine*, March 1932.

Graham, John, 'The Novels of Neil Gunn', *Edinburgh University: Jabberwock*, May 1948.

Hart, Francis Russell, 'The Hunter and the Circle: Neil Gunn's Fiction of Violence', *Studies in Scottish Literature*, 1963–4.

Lindsay, Maurice, 'Conversations With a Novelist', *Scottish Field*, May 1961, edited version of two conversations with Gunn recorded for the BBC in October 1959 and May 1960.

McCulloch, Margery, 'Neil M. Gunn: the Short Stories', *Scottish Literary Journal*, May, 1987.

_____ review of John Burns's *Celebration of the Light*, *Scottish Literary Journal*, Spring 1989.

McLeery, Alistair, 'The Genesis of the Green Isle of the Great Deep', *Studies in Scottish Literature*, XXII, (1987).

_____ Winds of War. Edited extracts from Gunn's 1939 Journal, *Scotsman*, 29 August 1987.

_____ 'The "Lost" Novel of Neil Gunn', *Studies in Scottish Literature*, Supplement 17 (Winter 1982). An examination of *The Poaching at

Grianan, serialized in the *Scots Magazine,* 1929, but – wisely – never published in book form.

Morgan, Edwin, 'The Louring Highlands', *Times Literary Supplement,* 3 December 1976. A review of some Gunn reissues.

Muir, Edwin, review of *The Serpent, Scots Magazine,* August 1943.

Pick, J. B., 'The Work of Neil Gunn', *Gangrel,* London, no. 2 (1945).

—— Memories of Neil Gunn, *Studies in Scottish Literature,* 1979.

—— A Tale of Two Anti-Utopias: Orwell's 1984, Gunn's Green Isle.

—— *Weekend Scotsman,* 17 December, 1984.

Reid, Alexander, 'The Theme is Man', *Scotland's Magazine,* July 1958.

Spence, Alan, 'Highland Zen', *New Edinburgh Review,* Spring 1982.

—— 'Celebrating the Light', *Cencrastus,* Summer 1988.

White, Kenneth, 'Zen and the Birds of Kentigern', *Cencrastus,* no. 11 (1983).

Index